ART THERAPIES

ART THERAPIES

DANIEL BROWN

Thorsons
An Imprint of HarperCollinsPublishers

Thorsons
An Imprint of HarperCollins*Publishers*
77–85 Fulham Palace Road,
Hammersmith, London W6 8JB

Published by Thorsons 1997
1 3 5 7 9 10 8 6 4 2

A catalogue record for this book
is available from the British Library.

ISBN 0 7225 3495 7

Printed and bound in Great Britain by
Caledonian International Book Manufacturing Ltd, Glasgow

TO MANDY

CONTENTS

ACKNOWLEDGEMENTS

Thank You to:
Sarah Holland for letting me contribute to the Bracton Centre art groups, Kim Suchet for her enthusiasm in co-running the Greenwich District Hospital groups, Simon Ings for ideas on art and SF, David Jane for deeply-felt courageous paintings, Jerome Carson for advice on de-stress, Padmal de Silva for discussions on literature, all the secretarial team at the Institute of Psychiatry for putting up with endless requests, Dr Janet Treasure for motivation, Kathy Morris, Catherine Marvell, Meg Rolleston and Brian McKenzie for training opportunities, John Drake for classical scholarship, John Turner for (nothing less than) multimedia genius, Nicola Cosgrave for advice on art and relationships, Cherry Boa for diagrammatic therapeutic techniques, Jo Boatman and Richard Anson at Cyberia for their Internet energies, Wanda Whiteley for Getting on With It, Carole Tonkinson for pushing on with me, Christina Digby for her tireless editorial work and skill, Myra Schneider for the poetry, Alison Combes for inspirational ideas and resources in the arts, the National Benefit Poetry Team: Dr Charlotte Wilson Jones, Dr Sara Majid, Richard Halward, and Ravi Wickremasinghe for into-the-night poetry analysis, and my colleagues, friends and family for continuous support and encouragement.

ACKNOWLEDGEMENTS

INTRODUCTION

> Every day look at a beautiful picture, read a beautiful poem, listen to some beautiful music, and if possible say some reasonable thing.
>
> JOHANN VON GOETHE

The heated argument had gone on and on, and was going nowhere. Hours had passed, and it was late at night. The woman I was arguing with left the room, then returned with a piece of yellow paper. On it was written a poem by Guillaume Apollinaire:

> 'Come to the edge.'
> 'No, we will fall.'
> 'Come to the edge.'
> 'No, we will fall.'
> They came to the edge.
> He pushed her, and they flew.

It had a very curious effect. I laughed. I considered. The poem totally changed how I had been thinking, and the argument was over.

This book is about changing yourself by working with the arts. I will show how looking at pictures, reading poems and stories, listening to music and watching drama can help you to feel better; and how to paint, perform, write and create music that will boost your morale and help you to problem-solve creatively. I will then explain how to apply these strategies to all areas of your life.

There are other art forms not described in this book: dance gives you enormous powers of expression, and connects directly with the body; photography is primarily concerned with how you perceive and represent the world. The techniques in this book can be applied to any therapeutic art form.

The benefits that flow from feeling more positive include: improved physical health, more energy, more fulfilling relationships, a clearer mind and, of course, greater happiness. Curiously, we often powerfully resist feeling good about ourselves, and stifle even the intention to move on. Remember, feeling bad helps nobody: you deserve to feel good.

The book contains many examples, and exercises, which involve creating and appreciating art. These demand work. I hope that you will try some of them. As the adage has it: 'It is not enough to know, you must do what you know.' The power of the exercises is revealed by their action.

When you start painting or writing, you are likely to become so engrossed in what you are doing, that you enjoy it. After doing the work, most people are quick to acknowledge an emotional transformation. If you try five exercises and none of them do anything for you, you can say they do not work. But if you do not try any of them, you will never know.

Many of the activities outlined in the book are fun and even playful. Some encourage non-logical thinking, with techniques for exploring and expressing both rational and non-rational thinking processes. You may find this difficult, because

Western culture is so preoccupied with being logical. For example, you may ask: why should I paint a picture? What possible use will that be to me? For now you will have to trust that painting a picture can and will change your mood, help you to understand yourself better, and design a more fulfilling life. The case studies in the book illustrate how the symbols people have created have helped them towards new goals.

WHY TURN TO THE ARTS?

Feeling sad? Read or write a poem! Feeling anxious? Look at or paint a picture! It sounds ridiculous, yet besides my own experiences, so many people – clients, doctors, therapists, friends, business leaders – have told me such impressive stories of personal development through artistic activities, that I really believe them to be an effective therapeutic force. By working systematically, focusing on the different elements of an art form, you can work through your emotions, find new ways of looking at difficult experiences, reshape the past and design a greater future.

At a conference on the use of arts in healing held at the Institute of Psychiatry in London, several long-term users of the mental health services told me how working with the arts had helped them to overcome what seemed like intractable problems, some of which had lasted for many years.

Arts have the power to access deep emotions: they can change the way you feel about the world and yourself. Actors have told me how they can feel, and almost see, drama unlocking emotions in an audience. Because of this, arts can facilitate rapid change, deep insights and a creative approach to living. Healing is concerned with bringing the body into a natural state of balance. The arts, whether by blending musical tones or groups of colours, achieve such a balance symbolically.

At the Withymoor village surgery in Dudley, England, the consulting rooms were painted in bright colours. The decor was so popular that the concept of using art to heal was extended. Now live music is played for mothers attending antenatal classes; colourful posters adorn the walls; theatre groups perform educational work in the waiting room; a local poet helps patients to write poems and prose about their problems; and artists make congratulations cards for every woman at the Withymoor practice on the birth of her child. The GP in charge, Dr Malcolm Rigler, says: 'I came to realize that the diagnosis of a single complaint always involved an understanding, and sometimes even an intervention in the culture, stories and traditions of the neighbourhood.'

I wonder how you are feeling right now. Maybe you are bright, active, in good condition, and ready to start the exercises. Maybe you are lethargic, or even depressed. Let me assure you that the methods in this book have helped a wide range of people: young people suffering from anorexia; the elderly; the long-term unemployed; people feeling dissatisfied with their careers, or feeling empty and devoid of emotion; and active, exuberant people who want even more energy. I have not yet met anybody who did not benefit from engaging in art therapies.

THINKING ABOUT ART

The primary purpose of this book is to encourage you to create arts for your self-development. In order to do this, you need to think about arts not only as ways of expressing thoughts and feelings to others, but as ways of developing symbols for change: symbols to help you alter and develop your feelings, your concept of self, and relationships with others.

PRINCIPLES OF ART THERAPIES

A non-judgemental attitude is crucial to allow the artistic part of you to flourish. Throughout your therapeutic work with arts, try to ignore criticism from yourself and others. The aim is to understand and change how you represent things to yourself, not to reach some ideal 'standard'. As the philosopher Søren Kierkegaard said: 'Only the truth that works is the truth for you.'

It is sad how often people are conditioned to believe that they cannot do things. So many people downplay themselves, saying things like: 'I can't draw,' or 'I can't play music.' Invariably, however, after a short time practising some form of art therapy, they find they can create in ways that satisfy them. A rule of mine is: 'Don't say: "I can't." Have a go at it, then ask: "How can I move on from here?"'

Develop a way of measuring your progress. You might count the number of words or pages written, pictures drawn or songs sung. Precisely how you measure your progress does not matter, but it is important to have a way of assessing what and how you are doing. This is not to berate yourself – it is a way of honestly giving yourself congratulation.

It is never too early or too late to start working with the arts. Remember, Sophocles produced some of his greatest plays when he was in his eighties; George Michael wrote his first songs when he was in his teens. As Alexander Pope said:

Too late? No, never is too late.
Unless the heart should cease to palpitate.

If you want to start, start now.

Many people think that they should face up to the 'real' world, and not be dreamers. But many of the things in the world we live in come from someone else's dreams. The light-bulb came from a dream of Thomas Edison's, which many respectable scientists of his time declared to be absurd. Your real world is shaped by your dreams. It is limiting to only focus on what is physically around you. Right now, you are surrounded by your dreams, hopes and visions of the present and future. Science fiction writer Simon Ings explains that visions of the future profoundly influence the way the future looks. The design of Japanese cars produced today are based on illustrations from 1950s American science fiction. So science fiction determined what happens now, in reality. This shows the importance of your imaginings: they are a solid platform on which to construct your reality. Of course, you don't want to be like the astronomer who always gazed at the moon, never looked at the road as he walked, and fell into a hole; or like Dr Pangloss, who asserted that he lived in 'the best of the best of all possible worlds', when his life was patently falling apart. Don't ignore the world around you, but don't ignore your dreams, either.

THE PAST, PRESENT AND FUTURE

We need to understand how events in the past influence the present. It is fascinating how we absorb experiences in our minds. Once internalized, they do not go away: a powerful experience of ten years ago can suddenly, unexpectedly even, be summoned into the present and relived with great intensity, affecting your beliefs, feelings, relationships and behaviour.

Using the arts, you can reshape or reframe past experiences so they have a positive impact on the present (and thereby the future). You can take the worst thing in the world, and turn it into something good. Instead of seeing the break-up of a relationship as a terrible happening, you can see it as providing new beginnings: it all depends on your perspective. And

perspective is under your control. What matters is not what
you experience, but how you see your experience.

CREATIVE INSPIRATION

How often we hear phrases like: 'It was only during her great-est despair that her true genius flourished.' Rubbish! The notion of the suffering artist is a false one. As Julia Cameron says in her book, *The Artist's Way*, 'In retrospect I am astound-ed I could let go of the drama of being a suffering artist. Noth-ing dies harder than a bad idea.'

The familiar story is that creative energy emerges from the shadow side of your personality. When you look at the lives of creative geniuses, you encounter a gallery of disturbed figures: a tormented Vincent Van Gogh severing his ear, a wild Fyodor Dostoevsky gambling himself into destitution. But you don't have to be despairing, tormented, demented or perverted to create. They are not necessary requirements or even useful components of the artistic process. Banish the moping genius, and develop a positive image to inspire you. Artists can and do produce from emotional balance and equilibrium.

It has been argued that while creativity channels trauma into symbols, such as a painting or a statue, it does not help to resolve pain. It is true that creating symbols alone does not nec-essarily resolve a trauma: the instances of disturbed artists repeating painful themes in their work testify to this. However, a healing process can occur using symbols, **provided there is a positive transformation of the symbol**. Paul McCartney described how Linda's recent battle with cancer influenced his latest music: 'A lot of my emotions from the recent difficult times are in [my album] one way or another. There were days when I would go off in a corner or take a walk and find myself putting a song together. It was my way of coping really.'

OBSERVING AND CREATING ART

Creating and appreciating art can both contribute to your development. They enhance each other: understanding other artists' methods of expression extends your own range of techniques, and working on expressing yourself helps you to understand the efforts of others. Transforming your emotions using symbols in art can be done by creating or appreciating.

When feelings are effectively explored and resolved in a work of art, there tends to be clarity of expression. Correspondingly, the most moving and inspiring artworks usually communicate strong feelings. A psychiatrist working on the National Benefit Poetry Project in the UK commented that in spite of her day-to-day exposure to suffering, some of the poems reduced her to tears, they were so moving. The judges, poets Ken Smith and Matthew Sweeney remarked that the best poems do not necessarily have outstanding technical virtuosity; however, in their view, the most stimulating poems have both feeling and order, which transform communication into art that inspires.

Usually, you become more involved with the things you do than the things you observe. So you will gain most by creating your own work. Drawing a stick figure, provided you are investing your feelings, is more powerful than studying a Leonardo painting in the Paris Louvre, because you are the artist. However, mechanically painting is less effective than wholeheartedly viewing an image, and actively engaging with a well-known poem has more emotional power than disinterestedly writing lines of verse.

So, in art therapy, you need to engage emotionally with the work, whether you are expressing or observing it; and the work must include a symbol of change. These two keys have the power to unlock your inner world, and develop it.

HOW ART THERAPIES WORK

To develop a complete mind:
Study the art of science;
Study the science of art.
Learn how to see.
Realize that everything connects to everything else.

LEONARDO DA VINCI

Art therapies excel when it comes to examining how you look at yourself and the world. Whether working with clay, words, or piano keys, an artist constructs a world of symbols that frees up emotions and ideas. We all have symbols which represent our thoughts and feelings – for example, a beautiful sunset might mean peace or sadness to you. How can art be used to change their meaning?

All therapies work on changing symbols or their significance within your mind. Art therapies help you to do this in two stages:

1. ENGAGING WITH A SYMBOL

To change an emotional state, the first thing you need to do is connect with it, otherwise all attempts at transformation will fail. It would be like pressing on the accelerator when the car is in neutral: no matter how fast the engine turns over, the car won't move. If you are working with a therapist, you need to trust her and feel safe, so that you dare to engage with your emotions.

Then you need to find a symbol that accords with your emotion. For example, if your mood is sombre, you might use music that begins heavy-heartedly. The symbol must be appropriate to the individual. A therapist must work to help you engage with the symbol. Some healers are brilliant at helping their clients to engage with very obscure symbols, and can generate deep changes in emotional state using something as unlikely as a handful of sand.

2. SYMBOLIC TRANSFORMATION

When you have chosen your symbol, you either follow how it metamorphoses (e.g. if you are listening to music, or watching a film); or, if you have created it yourself, you change it in a positive way. Without change, negative emotions fester.

It is important not to dwell too long on a symbol of negative mood, as you risk sinking into a down-hearted quagmire, and finding yourself stuck. However, if you try to make changes too rapidly, they may only be superficial and leave the negative emotions fundamentally unaltered.

If you feel low one morning, the best way to change your emotional state is to listen to music that moves you from ponderous feelings to a light, bright, energetic state. Listening to only moody, depressing music will not shift your state, and if you only listen to lively music, there is a good chance that your emotions will not connect with it.

A psychiatrist who was also a DJ adopted exactly this method. He discovered that if he started the evening with fast, high energy music, no one would dance. People milled around, disconnected from the music. So, he would sense the initial mood of the dancers, and play music relating to it, then slowly build up the pace and rhythm of the music to create a fantastic night of dancing.

Once change has occurred, it needs to be sustained, otherwise beliefs about the possibility of change can crumble. They need to be strengthened, so that you know you can control your feelings, avoid relapsing; and if you feel vulnerable again, repeat the exercise.

In 1974, psychologist Jerome Frank completed a classic analysis of how therapies work. He identified five core attributes of all successful therapies. They:

1) provide new learning opportunities at cognitive or experiential levels;
2) enhance hope of relief;
3) give success and mastery experiences (gaining control or understanding);
4) overcome a sense of alienation;
5) arouse emotions.

The art therapies accord naturally with these five key therapeutic elements.

1) They are very effective formats for **learning**: they help you to see new perspectives on situations, and offer stimulating methods for understanding adapting and memorizing. Art forms can connect with deep level thought processes, and thereby effect lasting emotional change.

Don was an anxious, irascible man in his mid-forties, who had oscillated for over twenty years between depression and addiction to drugs and alcohol. Unsuccessful treatments included tranquillizers, which made him more depressed, and psychotherapy, by which he felt frustrated and abandoned. He began art therapy after the break-up of a relationship; he was so sceptical that he thought: 'Why not? It might pass the time.' Surprisingly, he discovered that through painting, he could express feelings that he had kept bottled up for years. He was able to explore these feelings and learn that he had been engaged in repetitive cycles of self-destructive behaviour. He used the insights to reorganize his life, and later focused on more positive feelings about himself. When he finished therapy, he was free from addiction, happy with himself and more confident than he had been for many years.

2) Like other therapies, art therapies enhance **hope of relief** from mental suffering. Believing you can change and feel better is the first step. If someone thinks their chances of recovery are small, they are less likely to recover.

3) Art therapies give you experiences of **success** and **mastery**: creating a form of expression is in itself an achievement, and there is an intrinsic delight in accomplishing a picture or poem.

Writer Fiona Sampson spent 18 months as a writer-in-residence for the Isle of Wight health authority. Her brief was to work with children, acutely ill adults, and long-term psychogeriatric and hospice patients. During her residency, she identified that one of the reasons writing heals is because it transforms particular needs into something important and universal: something other people can read, a work of art. Instead of being a victim, you are someone with status: the patient becomes a writer.

4) A fundamental element of the arts is establishing **connection**. When you see a great picture, you connect with either the subject – whether it's a portrait, a time of day or a place – or the style – like an abstract painting by Mondrian. It

may reflect the way you structure your feelings, thoughts, or the world around you. When we sing songs, the upbeat rhythm of a tune can lift our spirits; slower melodies make us more dreamy.

The arts help you to reach and share powerful experiences and emotions. When a complex feeling or experience that is hard to relate to is depicted eloquently by an artist, the recognition can be deeply moving. The sense of being understood is one of the most powerful in therapy, and the phrase 'I understand' resonates throughout the great works of art.

5) Art forms – great pictures, fine plays and songs – **arouse powerful emotions**, from love and hate to fear and excitement. Lasting change – the kind of change you aim for in art therapies – occurs when you are able to repeat and understand your feelings, and accept them.

The arts should be applied accurately and systematically in therapy. Effective therapeutic art forms should:

- aim for lasting effect, so that they do not only change, but maintain change – they should not be too dry and logical as this prevents you from processing your emotions;
- increase your sense of hope substantially – overcoming obstacles and surviving unbearable pain show that you have successful coping strategies;
- provide success experiences by helping you to understand and overcome challenges;
- transform emotions using relevant symbols. The main choice of medium – painting, drama, poetry, stories or music – is whatever you prefer;
- facilitate emotional arousal to process deep-level emotions.

PRINCIPLES OF ART THERAPIES

SYMBOLS AND IMAGES

As a teenager, I thought I was pretty cool sporting a picture of a washing machine on my T-shirt with the caption: 'Mean and moody: I feel like a lost sock in the laundromat of oblivion.' While I did not feel great about myself at the time, the image was striking. When I grew up a bit, I saw that images are powerful ways of capturing emotional states. This has encouraged me to think up more positive images.

To master the mind, you need to lock what you know of your emotions, experiences and beliefs into vivid symbols. Symbols can hold enormous quantities of intellectual and emotional information with great succinctness. Art therapies create a tool kit for the mind. You can use them to produce a stock of empowering symbols to help you overcome obstacles that prevent you achieving your full potential. First, using the exercises in this book, you need to construct visual, acoustic and sensory symbols in your mind. Then I will encourage you to illustrate these in paintings, poems, music, stories and drama. The act of externalizing symbols reinforces them in the mind.

Symbols can be more powerful than verbal affirmations (such as repetition of the phrase: 'I am strong'), because they connect with a more basic level in your mind. Think of the difference between the single word 'strong' and the image of the Niagara Falls exploding down a three hundred metre chasm. Instead of thinking: 'I should be more optimistic,' try invoking a vivid, optimistic sun to shine upon all your actions. If you have obstacles to overcome, construct bridges in your mind to cross over them, bombs to destroy them, or turn yourself into a swallow that can swoop and glide effortlessly over them. What is your personal symbol of success? What symbols would make you smile, feel more loving, or become more organized?

Imagine a prism, and see your confusion as a diffuse beam of light. A prism separates white light into clear strands of different colours. Symbols in art can do the same for your feelings – separate them out so they become more manageable.

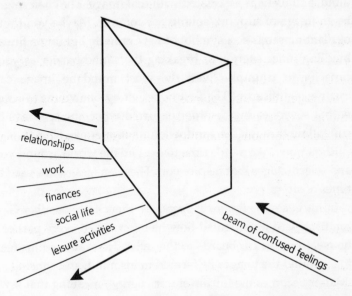

relationships

work

finances

social life

leisure activities

beam of confused feelings

We attach all sorts of thoughts and feelings to symbols. Advertisers especially are aware of this: it means that they can turn the act of drinking a cup of coffee into something full of sex and glamour, or associate a car tyre with the feeling of confidence. Marketing expert and author of *Superbrands*, Marcel Knobil, described how the company Dulux wanted to communicate in a shorthand way that their paint was durable, warm and cosy. They used the image of a sheep dog, which succinctly encapsulates all these qualities. The symbol has been so effective that the company has remained faithful to it for many years.

You can transform your everyday world into symbols, and use them as a basis for changing your view of life. The great artists are celebrated in part for looking at things in new ways. Think about how you internalize the world around you, and construct symbols. If you are sitting on a chair, close your eyes and think of the chair. You will have an image of it in your mind, and feelings associated with that image. The chair might be an image of support, solidity, or comfort. Maybe you think of planting seeds as a symbol of new growth; lighting a fire as kindling inner energy; or breaking the sound barrier as your capacity to triumph. Even the most mundane image can assume significance. The first hope felt by one young woman with a severe eating disorder occurred when she saw rays of sun falling through the window on a summer morning.

Right now, take a little time to explore the world around you and select images that inspire you. These images can be used at times of stress.

In his book *The Poetics of Space*, the French philosopher Gaston Bachelard investigated how he internalized every part of a house, from the cupboards to the cellar. He examined his feelings around the images he formed in his mind, and concluded: 'Matter becomes the mirror of our energy', meaning that if we view ourselves in a positive way, the world around us becomes empowering.

Gerald Epstein describes his meeting with imagery therapist Colette Aboulker-Muscat in his book *Healing Visualization*. He was explaining to her the similarities between imagery and Sigmund Freud's technique of free association. In Freud's exercise, the analyst tells the client to imagine them both riding on a train: the client looks out of the window and describes everything he or she sees.

Mme Aboulker-Muscat responded by asking: 'In what direction does the train go?' Dr Epstein was caught short by this question. He wondered what it had to do with therapy. Worried that he might give the wrong answer, he cautiously replied that trains go in a horizontal direction, and he made a horizontal gesture with his hand. But Mme Aboulker-Muskat made an upwards movement with her forearm, saying: 'Well, what if the direction were changed to this axis?'

At this moment, Epstein felt profound self-recognition. It was a revelation to him: 'The vertical movement seemed to lift me from the horizontal hold of the given, the ordinary patterns of everyday cause and effect. I leapt into freedom and I saw that the task of therapy – the task of being human – was to help realize freedom, to go beyond the given … to our capacity to renew and recreate. That is what imagery, I have come to learn, makes possible.'

Effective imagery connects emotions and sensations with images. Feelings are intrinsically connected with images. For example, what image do you associate with feeling angry? Constructing images in your mind allows you to generate completely new responses to situations and problems. While the mental pictures in your mind do not exist outside your imagination, they have energy that can be used make real changes in the external world.

Here is a visualization for exploring loving feelings. See how these images make you feel as you read and visualize the following text.

Breathe in and out deeply three times. See yourself walking along the beach of an island. You are on your own, it is sunny and warm, and a gentle breeze blowing along the coast leaves you feeling calm and relaxed. At the edge of the beach is a small sailing boat. You climb onboard and untie the knot in the rope that moors it to a tree on the shore. Now you are free to use the sea breeze to direct your boat in the direction that you choose. You are on course for the island where your lover is waiting for you. Deep down, you know which direction to take. As you sail out to sea, the wind becomes stronger. You use it to make a steady, fast course. The wind in your face is cool, while the sun shines brightly. In the distance, you see the outline of the island you are heading for. Enjoy the sensations of lightness and swiftness as your craft glides over the water towards your destination. You near the coast. On the shore of the island, you see your lover, who, smiling, recognizes you. You moor the boat by the shore, and your lover enters the boat. Now you turn the boat around, and the two of you set off out to sea.

SYMBOLS AND HYPNOSIS

Symbols can be used in hypnosis to reach the deeper levels of the mind. In their book *Hypnotherapy: A Practical Handbook*, Helmut Karle and Jennifer Boys describe how hypnosis uses symbols of descent – such as going down in a lift, on an escalator or staircase – to reach the deeper levels of a person's mind. Images of distance can also be used. Thus the hypnotized person can 'picture himself lying comfortably on a raft or in a small boat, drifting down a river, noting that as he drifts further and further (away from the everyday world), the river gets wider and wider, and he is further and further away from the bank on either side, while he feels a gentle rocking motion as he drifts gently towards and into an idyllic inner world.'

IDENTITY AND ART

How you view yourself and other people is at the centre of how you perceive the world. The arts can help you think differently about yourself. Consider this excerpt from a story I wrote.

One late frosty winter's afternoon, as You and I were deep in a quiet and thoughtful walk, I wandered off the track over to the edge of the river. I felt a bit sombre, and I said so to You.

'I wish I were more confident,' I said.

'Had more confidence, you mean,' said You.

I was irritated by the smug manner of You at this point, and I was about to say so when I noticed something strange in the left hand of You. It was a perfectly round lump, about the size of a tennis ball and in the gently darkening evening it gave out a soft, luminous yellow light.

'What is that stuff?' I asked.

'It's confidence,' You said.

'Yeah, right,' I said. I tried to snatch the glowing ball away, but when I did so, a piece of it broke off. I opened my hand and it no longer glowed.

So I scooped up a clod of earth from the ground and held the lump high in the air.

'That's not confidence,' said You.

'How do You know?' I asked.

'Because,' You laughed and touched the lump of earth.

It hardened, then shattered into small pieces. I threw the pieces away.

'How do I make confidence?' I asked.

'From experience,' You said.

'Where do I get that?'

'It's everywhere: all around you,' said You. You picked up some pieces of earth, then followed the direction of the wind over to a bush, and plucked off some of the leaves.

You made a little bundle out of this and presented it to I.

'How ridiculous!' I exclaimed.

You smiled.

'What am I supposed to do with this dirt?' I demanded. 'Do what you need to do,' said You and walked away, following the course of the river.

I clenched the bundle in anger, and then marched back to the village. The little houses with chimneys merrily smoking seemed horribly cosy and I felt lonely, isolated and cold. I squashed the bundle in one hand.

An old woman with grey hair in a bun walked past, dressed in a dark black coat.

'What are you doing standing here on your own?' she said. 'You'll catch a terrible cold.'

'I'm making confidence,' I said.

'Oh, tut, tut,' she said. 'Oh, tut, tut, tut.' And she walked off.

I stood looking at the strange shapes of the smoke pouring out of the chimneys for at least ten minutes.

Time passed. A shower of sparks flew out of one of the chimneys into the dark sky. A startled black crow lurched off its trajectory and flew towards the moon.

From the far end of the road appeared a small moving shadow. It grew and spread across the pavement. The shadow had four legs. It grew larger. Then its owner appeared. It was a little black cat which trotted lightly along the street. It stopped and stretched.

The cat looked directly ahead, as if it knew something. I smiled. I took out the bundle of leaves and fragments and looked at it.

In the centre of the squashed little heap, something glowed.

Stories like this are ways of re-viewing yourself. Think about what the symbols (the glowing ball, the clod of earth, the old woman) mean to you. Did you connect with them and engage emotionally? If not, what symbols would have worked more effectively for you?

Everyone should have complete jurisdiction and absolute freedom over their identity, yet it is so central that freedom is potentially terrifying. Many people spend very little time considering who they really are. How would you feel if I asked you, right now, to say who you think you really are? Could you define yourself in a paragraph? How would you like to define yourself? And how would you then go on to re(de)fine yourself?

Draw a sketch of your identity in a 10 by 10 cm square, or a circle. Drawing often frees up alternative ways of looking at yourself. How do you feel about having the freedom to put anything at all in the square? What is it important to put in the square? Do you have enough space, or too much space? Study the picture for a few minutes, then add some characteristics you would like to have, that you don't see yourself as already having.

All therapies are about according with negative thoughts and feelings, and moving towards more positive ones. The process by which human spirit and energy flows into symbols is fascinating, and best understood by **doing**.

PREPARING TO
DO ART THERAPIES

The work of the artist is to heal the soul.

KATHLEEN RAINE

Most people do not like problems: they run away from them, and try to avoid them. And life is full of them! On the other hand, problems are a scientist's food and drink. Nobel prize-winning physicist Richard Feynman spent his life hunting out problems.

One way to change your attitude towards problems is to develop a creative attitude towards them. Imagine solving your problems in the same way as you might splash paint over a canvas. It would be pretty light-hearted and fun, wouldn't it?

It is important to have a symbol for your creativity. Be careful: it must be useful, like a helpful car-mechanic, not a destructive shrieker leading you to your doom. If it is a barrel of water that gathers the rain of experiences of the day, it might run dry. If it is an inexhaustible, everlasting inspirational spring, it will never dry up.

THE HEALING WAVE,
A CENTRAL SYMBOL

One element of all the art forms we have examined is a sense of harmony – there is a way in which everything has its place. Even the painful elements of life can make sense, be ordered, organized, integrated and become acceptable. This is a fundamental component of the healing process.

A useful core symbol is a healing wave that moves through you and alters your perception of your experiences. When it runs through you, you are healed. You may have had the extraordinary experience of the unbearable suddenly becoming bearable. Nothing about the situation has altered, but somehow, in your internal representation of how things are, you can cope with it, and move on. Something inside has changed. This wave of transformation can move unexpectedly through you, and it can also be within your control.

Visualize the motion of this healing wave, whether you choose the image of a wave on the sea, or a tiny ripple spreading out over a clear lake, or a sound wave travelling through the air.

You might find an alternative image of a lens useful, through which you can choose to focus on good things.

Devise some core positive symbols for yourself. Begin by assembling as many motifs as you can. Try to combine visual and auditory types of art, so that you use all your senses.

SEVEN WAYS OF ACCESSING AND ENHANCING YOUR CREATIVITY

1. LOOK AFTER YOURSELF

This may sound trite, but in order to be creative, it helps to be in a relaxed, free-wheeling state of mind. Meditation is useful for this, as is taking breaks away from the hustle and bustle of everyday life. Make sure you have an hour to yourself now and again, without demands or interruptions, where **you** can decide whether to have music playing or silence, electric lighting or candles. With the support of your family or housemates, this should be possible.

2. BREAK ESTABLISHED PATTERNS

Do something different: say hi to a stranger; walk a different way home; see a film you would not normally see. If you don't listen to music, go to a concert; if you usually listen to classical music, try a rock concert. Visit an art gallery; buy a book on architecture; try a new kind of food. Extend the boundaries of what you do. Breaking your routine can be liberating!

> Extend the boundaries of what you do.
> Exceed your greatest hopes – go further still:
> Break all that can't be done like sticks into
> A fuel that bursts to flames upon your will.

3. ENJOY CREATIVE RELATIONSHIPS

Freud described creativity as a sublimated expression of sexual urges in a socially acceptable form. Some people say they are more creative when they are not in a sexual relationship, because energy which they otherwise divert into relationships is used creatively. But Dr Gayle Delaney, author of the excellent *Sexual Dreams: Why We Have Them and What They Mean*, asserts

that: 'This is not a question of a sexual energy drain, but rather an interpersonal problem that drains both time and energy in general. Depending on its nature and quality, a relationship can be an example of a creative endeavour or a siphon of creative energy.' Dr Delaney proposes that a healthy, more open sexuality would enrich our creativity, and that we can use our dreams to encourage a mutual enrichment of our creative and sexual lives.

If being in a relationship seems to decrease your creative output, think of your creativity as a fire: when you heap a lot of coal on it, the flames are no longer visible, but soon the new coal catches light, and provides an even greater surge of heat.

4. USE YOUR DREAMS

While you sleep, you create images that are often incomprehensible to your conscious mind, but some of the greatest ideas and discoveries have been inspired by dreams. Look into your thoughts and feelings about your dreams. Think about:

- the characters – are they mysterious prowlers, horses, your ex, or your boss?
- the setting
- the objects in your dream – identify them, then free associate, i.e. note whatever comes into your mind when you think of each one
- the actions in the dream – who did what, when?

If you think a dream is uninteresting, or decide to think about it later, you may be resisting remembering it.

It does not matter where you are or what you are doing, there is always something going on around and within you. Use your senses to respond to your environment: look for patterns in the shapes and colours around you, and rhythms in the sounds you hear – even in the noise of the traffic.

The philosopher Roland Barthes had an apartment overlooking a busy Paris road. Night after night he could hear the traffic, and it infuriated him. He could not sleep. It never ceased. It annoyed him more and more: he was becoming exhausted and his work was suffering. Then, one night, it dawned on him that the sound of traffic was the sound of other people, of humanity. From then on, the traffic no longer troubled him, and he had no difficulty sleeping.

6. TRY ALL THE ART FORMS

It is important to explore all the art forms, to experiment with different ways of seeing things. People are often classified as 'visual' or 'verbal' – as good at one thing but not another. This pigeonholing is restrictive, unproductive and in all likelihood, not based on the truth. We choose how much energy to invest in developing each area of ourselves, so some areas will need more work than others.

If you practise different arts, you will become more adept at all of them. It is like running: as you become fitter at running, does your swimming or walking get worse? Of course not – running helps you to develop your other skills and improves your overall fitness. Likewise, toning up your drawing 'muscles' will not hinder your writing abilities – it is likely to improve them, even if you do not consider drawing to be your forte (yet).

The writer Goethe filled his mind with as many symbols as he could, to help him to develop his vision and powers of expression. His mind became so imbued with images that he wrote one day: 'As I glided over the lagoons in the brilliant sunshine and saw the gondoliers in their colourful costumes, gracefully poised against the blue sky as they rowed with easy strokes across the light green surface of the water, I felt I was looking at the latest and best painting of the Venetian school.'

The next time you write a poem, create visual metaphors to enhance your writing, such as: 'my passion is like a red blossom'. The next time you paint, focus your mind on more verbal ideas. The aim is to make the movement from the verbal to the visual more fluid. It may help to literally focus on one concept as a word and then express this pictorially, for example: paint grief, or excitement. Consider that Picasso's portraits were influenced by something as incongruous as Einstein's theory of relativity!

Allow creativity to permeate every area of your life. Your business letters or brochures might benefit from a new design; acting techniques might strengthen your conversational skills; composing a story might help you make better presentations. As Robert Henri said in his book *The Art Spirit*: 'When the art spirit is alive in any person, whatever his kind of work may be, he becomes an inventive, healing, doing, self-expressive creature.'

7. BEWARE OF CRITICISM

Most people start painting when they are very young. You throw colours and shapes on a piece of paper, make a mess and nobody seems to mind. You even get praised. It's fun. Then you grow up, and the freedom disappears. The critics arrive and teach you how to be ashamed of yourself and your work. Most people have not been taught how to criticize constructively. I believe the education system should teach everyone how to give effective feedback.

Whenever I am asked to judge an artistic work, I find three things I like, and suggest one area for development. When you think about it, you can always find something that is good, even in a song or film you do not like. The creator of the work goes away, and considers whether they agree with my comments or not. Usually, they return. Lo and behold, their next work has progressed! If as children we had coaches to encourage us, rather than instil a dread of failure, a lot more people of all ages would dare to be creative.

So, encourage yourself! Don't let your internal critic dominate. You may like to visualize your critic as a small bug-eyed monster, which you can squash. Find an alternative figure to internalize, and inspire you, an intrepid explorer perhaps. Then exercise the parts of yourself that are less developed. For years, I did not think I understood music. I felt foolish because I could not comprehend the spidery graphics of a musical score. Only recently have I embarked on understanding how to read and compose music. I am progressing in this, and enjoying it. Expect a tune, soon!

Nobel prize-winning writer Herman Hesse used never to give bad reviews of books. If he read a book he did not like, he simply would not review it. All his reviews were positive.

START TODAY. START
THIS HOUR. START NOW.

> Couldn't everyone's life become a work of art? Why
> should the lamp or the house be an art object, but not
> our life?
>
> MICHEL FOUCAULT

'Now' is a magical word. It constantly disappears and is end-
lessly renewed – like a continuous supply of money waiting
to be spent, which is worthless if not used immediately. If you
want to make objects or images, until you start, you have nothing to develop. Nothing doubled is still nothing. Suspend your
fears and judgements, and let ideas and feelings flow into your
creations. Patterns will emerge which you can develop later.
Aim to ally your emotions with the symbols that you create,
and focus on the process of change, on feeling better. Your present actions fall like rocks into the past, but stand as stepping
stones to the future.

Being creative is like getting fit: it takes regular practice. With
continuous effort you become leaner, faster and stronger. Creative fitness releases energy that you can use in other areas of
your life.

There is no point in waiting for inspiration. If you have prac-
tised when it arrives, you will be ready to catch your thoughts

as they fly out. Creative habits are essential to stop them running away. Although your output may flow more easily at some times than others, it is crucial that you work on yourself even when you do not feel like it. This is usually when you benefit most.

It does not mean that you should not have fun with your art. The trick is to make creating an enjoyable habit. Lounging around, watching hours of television might seem fun, but it usually brings unsatisfying slothful feelings and few rewards. Creativity requires effort, but can be enjoyable.

SIX WAYS OF GETTING STARTED

1. ESTABLISH A ROUTINE

Set times which you will devote to your creativity, and which are inviolable: discipline is a form of love. Of course, if your house is burning, you do not carry on regardless and combust, but if a television show begins, maybe it has to go by the wayside.

2. FEAR NOT THE BLANK PAGE

For many artists – writers, poets, musicians and dramatists – the blank page is a potent symbol of horror. They become unnerved by it: they break into a sweat and start trembling. This is so unnecessary. The blank page can be exciting! It offers an opportunity: anything can be thrown at it. Write or draw anything. If you think that what you write, compose or doodle is rubbish, it doesn't matter – eventually a theme will emerge.

Artwork enables you to process mental blocks, and reveal the source. The best tool for overcoming writer's block, for example, is writing – just sitting down and going through the motions. If you want to paint, then paint. If you feel sad, paint through the sadness, then move on to the theme you want to focus on. If you compose or play music, play through numbing feelings towards more meaningful ones. You are a creative person, and have wonderful resources at your disposal. Like a hungry chef in a restaurant, make yourself a sandwich!

3. ENJOY YOURSELF!

It is important to have some fun while you are looking at your emotions, your self, your relationship with the world, the past, present and future. So often, people look at issues in a heavy, serious, sometimes even tragic way. But a chief ingredient of great inventions is a sense of fun.

Take a look at your future. Many people dread the future, so they choose not to think about it, and as a consequence, do not enjoy the future they would like. You can imagine your future now. In your mind, you can create vivid pictures about the future using all your senses. Although we take this completely for granted, it really is quite incredible. What great stories could you make about your future? What amazing twists and turns could you devise that would ensure ever greater levels of excitement, comedy, passion, and joy in your life? What musical score unfolds in unexpected ways from where you are now? How could you have more fun with your future? Is the future a long and winding road? Draw in some enjoyable excursions.

4. BANISH YOUR INNER CRITIC

Art therapies are concerned with the feelings evoked by an artwork. The emotional transformation achieved is more important than the artistic product itself.

Nevertheless, your inner critic will attempt to foil you in clever, cunning ways. It will fill your mind with negative opinions about yourself, and inhibit your creativity. It will attempt to prevent you from working with this book; dismiss your creative ideas as indulgent, silly, time-wasting or childish; tell you

PRINCIPLES OF ART THERAPIES

that your music does not compare with your friends'; that your poems are not up to Shakespeare's. Somehow, you have to beat this critic. But to begin with, it is very difficult to ignore. Think of yourself as a car engine: it doesn't matter if the engine starts with a growl, purr or whisper – what matters is that it starts.

5. BE DISCERNING ABOUT FEEDBACK

If you are at the start of a creative phase and you wish to share your work, show it only to people who will give positive feedback. At a later stage, if you are interested in more detailed criticism, negative feedback may help you to refine your artworks. But at the outset, it can stymie and kill off creative ideas at their birth.

Great artists are adept at absorbing valid criticism and politely disregarding critics who miss the mark. Michelangelo, the great Italian sculptor, was commissioned by the Head of the Florentine Republic, Piero Solderini, to carve a figure from a block of marble. The six metre high block of marble had been standing neglected for some time in the Office of Works. Another artist named Simone da Fiesole had begun carving it, but had botched the work so badly that he had ruptured the block and bored a hole where the legs would have been.

Michelangelo carefully measured the block. He calculated that he would be able to carve a satisfactory figure from the marble by fitting its posture to the shape of the stone. He created a wax model of the figure, then, after erecting a partition of planks and trestles around the marble, he worked on it continuously, without letting anyone see it.

When it was finished, Piero Solderini came to see the statue. Standing below the sculpture, he remarked casually that he thought the nose was too thick. Michelangelo was used to handling criticism and knew the importance of satisfying the critics' need to appear well informed. He saw that the Head of

State was standing below his work, leaped onto his statue and took hold of a chisel with his left hand, together with some of the marble dust lying on the planks. Tapping lightly with the chisel, he let the dust fall little by little, without altering anything. Then he looked down at Solderini.

'Now look at it,' requested Michelangelo.

Solderini looked up at the statue.

'Ah, that's much better,' Solderini said. 'Now you've really brought it to life.'

Michelangelo climbed down from the statue, feeling almost sorry for the posturing critic. The sculpture was Michelangelo's *David*. It has put in the shade every other statue in the history of mankind. The grace of the figure and the serenity of its pose have never been surpassed.

6. MAKE A CREATIVE CONTRACT

If you are writing a book, having a rule that insists you write one page every day without fail is usually much more fruitful than doing the occasional twenty page splash, because at the end of three weeks, there they are: twenty-one pages at least. Should a shower of inspiration fall on you, that is a bonus, but you are not reliant on it.

You could sign the contract below, or use it as a basis for one of your own. It is very simple, but please think carefully before signing. You may want to read through this book before committing yourself, but I urge you to return and sign it! It will work as much as you empower it to work. You have to make sure that you adhere to the terms. You are the judge, jury and enforcement system – that's quite a responsibility!

CONTRACT

For the next three weeks, starting on

_____

I will create/study

_____

pages of

_____

for

_____

hours per day.

The themes will be:

_____

_____

_____

My goal in doing this is:

_____

I hereby declare that I shall abide by the terms
of this contract.

Signature _____

Date _____

Many people like to collect their paintings, or photographs of objects they have made, in a notebook, so that they can easily refer to their collection of symbols. It is also a record of personal development. If any of your work contains material that is especially sensitive to you, either find a safe place to store it, or destroy it. If you store your text, music or graphics on a computer, remember that most systems allow you to password protect your files.

WHAT IF YOU CREATE
SOMETHING DISTURBING?

It is not wrong to create disturbing images: one of the purposes of art therapies is to access powerful feelings. Disturbing emotions should not be ignored or repressed. The aim is ultimately to make the feelings containable, so what matters is how you frame them. It is not the feelings themselves but the meanings we attach to them which are important. A feeling of guilt, for example, can be a basis for personal development, by indicating where our standards have been contradicted; loneliness may be a signal to connect with people.

However, if symbols you have created disturb you, you may need to ask why. A garish visual image or a loud chaotic sound that does not appeal to you may indicate that there are parts of yourself that need attention. Art therapies are not used to linger on negative feelings, but to change them.

SHOULD YOU SHOW
YOUR WORK TO OTHERS?

Many people never show their work to anyone, whilst others enjoy sharing their art. What matters is that you do what is right for you. If you have produced art of emotional significance to you, be careful in the first instance at least to show it to people who will be sensitive to this. You might like to join a group of people who are also interested in art therapies, to motivate and support you. The people there are more likely to appreciate the value of your work, but you should never feel under pressure to share it.

SHOULD YOU WORK
ON SEVERAL ART FORMS AT A TIME?

It is useful to practise or observe more than one kind of art, to experiment with different ways of seeing things. People are often classified as 'visual' or 'verbal' – as good at one thing but not another. This pigeonholing is restrictive, unproductive and in all likelihood, untrue. We choose how much energy to invest in developing each area of ourselves, so some areas will need more work than others.

PAINTING

> Painting is a blind man's profession. He paints not what he sees, but what he feels, what he tells himself about what he has seen.
>
> PABLO PICASSO

Some time ago, I worked with an art group in a psychiatric hospital. It was supervised by a client who was also an art teacher. A group of clients had painted a series of pictures which were taped up on the wall.

The consultant psychiatrist walked into the art room and began to talk about the 'underlying psychopathologies'. The art teacher looked coolly at the psychiatrist. 'Never, ever analyse what a picture means,' she said. 'The picture is what it is. And that's the end of it.'

While much can be learned from studying paintings, a non-judgemental attitude is vital for creativity to flourish. You must be careful, particularly with your own works, how you analyse them. If you are critical, you will block your powers of creative expression.

HOW PAINTING THERAPY WORKS

Paintings and drawings have awesome power to generate and resonate with feelings. When I saw Edvard Munch's 'The Scream' for the first time, I was filled with shock and almost relief that such a terrible, deep feeling had been captured and set on canvas. In contrast, many of Manet's pictures have a soft, serene, restful quality. His beautiful oil paintings of shimmering haystacks on a summer's day, and the cathedral at Rouen, evoke warmth and the soft feeling of the summer. Such pictures are not necessarily intrinsically therapeutic, but they do have therapeutic potential, because they can connect with the viewer's emotions.

One woman in her twenties, trapped in a deferential, subservient relationship with her ill mother, painted a picture which revealed a blazing fury of which she was unaware until a friend commented on it. As she explored her feelings of anger, the relationship improved.

Paintings can show you new ways of looking at the world, yourself and your situation. In your own paintings, your inner world and outer reality fuse. They can help you to determine whether you need to change the world, or change yourself.

How do you describe your work on a daily basis? If it's a drag, how might it become a spree on a ski? If it's getting you down, how might it give you a lift? Draw a pulley system to convert some of the downward-pulling energy into an uplifting force.

By drawing the world as you see it, or as you would like it to be, you can order your feelings. Making images of how you would like things to be, helps you to control the way you see the world. While you paint, you can move from representing your feelings to transforming them – creating a new outlook by viewing a situation from a new perspective.

Buddhists and Hindus had this idea in mind when they created mandala symbols. A mandala is a sacred diagram symbolizing the universe. It can be imagined in the mind or drawn on paper, and is used for meditation and visualization. It is typically a circle enclosing a square containing a symbol.

SUITABILITY

Painting is effective for problems requiring flexible thinking and intuitive solutions, and for finding ways out of vicious circles. This is because painting exercises mostly the right side of the brain, and prevents the more logical left side of the brain from dominating. The left side of the brain controls and orders things, which is useful, but too much rigorous, logical control can impede the flow of creative ideas. It is useful to exercise the right side of the brain when goal-setting, because it does not impede you with 'logical' constraints, and allows you to think about what you really want to aim for, not what you think you ought to.

Cognitive Analytic Therapy is a short-term psychotherapy which is used to treat clients with fragmented personalities very successfully. A central component is the 'diagrammatic reformulation' of the client's situation. Even when a vicious circle of behaviour is identified, it is very difficult to change. Drawing the cycle makes the situation clear at a much deeper and more intuitive level of the brain. Diagrams can communicate the need for change in ways that words cannot.

In his book *Love, Medicine and Miracles*, Dr Bernie Siegel tells how he asks all new cancer patients to draw a picture of themselves, their disease and the white blood cells eliminating the disease, using crayons of all the colours in the rainbow. In his view: 'Such drawings bypass verbal descriptions and get to the universal symbolic language of the unconscious. When we communicate in visual ways, we tell the truth, because we can't manipulate the language as well.'

TECHNIQUES USED IN PAINTING

Shape, colour, light and shade are united in nature, but they are distinct elements of a painting.

COLOUR

Colour can both express and shape emotions. Some of the metaphors we use to express feelings derive from colours: people feel 'blue', or they are naively 'green'; politicians are 'dull' or 'grey'. The painter Wassilly Kandinski said: 'Colour is the keyboard, the eyes are the hammers, the soul is the piano with many strings. The artist is the hand that plays, touching one key or another purposively, to cause vibrations in the soul.'

Tone – the quality or shade of a colour – can be used to create balance and harmony: areas of dark can be balanced by areas of light. Goethe cites the Italian painter Veronese's ability to 'create harmony through a skilful distribution of light and shade and local colours.' The Italians named this chiaroscuro. Light and dark can be used to illustrate mood, and to highlight different feelings and actions.

COMPOSITION

The artist decides which objects to leave out, which to use, and how to arrange them on the canvas. When you look at a painting, think about how the shapes and colours are arranged. In landscape paintings, look at the lines and shapes of the woods and fields, and see how they create balance. A landscape stretching for miles, a variety of woods and fields, or the bold rocky features of a cliff inspire the mind with patterns. Horizontal and vertical lines in a picture can radiate tension and discomfort or stability and peace.

PERSPECTIVE

Perspective is a way of creating the illusion of three dimensions on a flat surface. The technique uses straight lines that converge at a 'vanishing point' about two thirds of the way up a picture: think of the two sides of a railway line converging on the horizon. The term 'find a different perspective on the situation' is so familiar that it is easy to ignore its pictorial origins.

'THE STARRY NIGHT'

Van Gogh's 'The Starry Night' depicts a small village at night. Twelve fiery swirling stars illuminate the darkness. If you focus on the picture for a while, you will notice that:

- the colours are intense and vibrant, with strong contrasts between the bright yellows of the stars and the blue/black sky, which balance each other out;
- the dark tones have a sombre mood – this is broken up by the light of the stars, which illuminates a hill in the distance;
- the way the painting is composed means that you focus on the stars;
- the lines in the picture exude a sense of harmony.

LOOKING AT PAINTINGS YOURSELF

Visit a gallery and select the picture which touches you most.

- How do the colours affect your mood?
- Do you concentrate more on certain colours than others?
- Do the tones make you feel lighter or darker inside?
- How are the colours and tones balanced in the composition?
- Does the geometry of the picture symbolize the structure of something else which you can identify?
- Does the painting change your emotions in a positive way?
- If not, what kinds of images and colours do you need for this to happen?

Here are three suggestions of paintings for you to look at to begin with: if you can't get to the original, you should be able to find them on a poster or a postcard, or in a book.

- 'Waterlilies' by Claude Monet – soft, subtle paintings that highlight a sense of beauty; soft greens and lilacs are relaxing in a dreamy way.
- 'Where are we going?' by Gauguin – the questing figures are in different symbolic poses and demonstrate different viewpoints on life at different times.

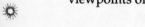

- 'Dance One' by Henri Matisse – this vast picture has a circular motion and achieves harmony using only four colours.

USING PAINTING TO SET GOALS

In art therapy seminars for business, I use a painting exercise to help clients set goals. The aim is to let the mind freewheel, and not be impeded by logical constraints. The clients start by asking themselves: what do I want out of my life? What do I want to achieve? What do I want to be? What are my personal, professional, business and community goals?

They then do a means–end analysis, which involves drawing arrows from each goal to the means necessary to achieve it. For example, if the goal is to buy your own house, it may require a means of earning over £20k per annum. The client takes four steps back, as in the following example:

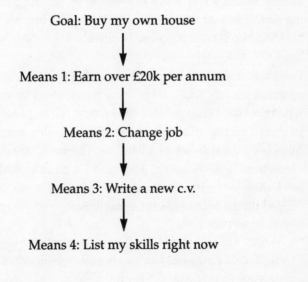

Goal: Buy my own house

↓

Means 1: Earn over £20k per annum

↓

Means 2: Change job

↓

Means 3: Write a new c.v.

↓

Means 4: List my skills right now

The fourth means is a simple one that can be acted upon immediately. This is in itself an extremely powerful exercise, and the use of art therapies extends it.

When the exercise has been done in writing, the clients illustrate all their goals and means. Arrows become rocket ships blasting off towards goals; cricket balls hurtle over boundaries towards success; flourishing trees illustrate wellbeing and security. The pictures are exciting and fun to do, and most importantly, they are memorable. They lock the goals unforgettably into people's minds. The person whose goal was a relationship might not recall the arrow diagram, but I doubt if she will forget the image of herself dancing with her lover through a universe of multi-coloured stars.

CASE STUDIES

An engineer who had a tense relationship with her boss at work released some of her frustration by painting a cartoon of the situation with caricatures. It channelled her normal angry reaction into something more positive.

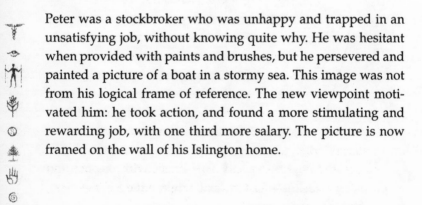

Peter was a stockbroker who was unhappy and trapped in an unsatisfying job, without knowing quite why. He was hesitant when provided with paints and brushes, but he persevered and painted a picture of a boat in a stormy sea. This image was not from his logical frame of reference. The new viewpoint motivated him: he took action, and found a more stimulating and rewarding job, with one third more salary. The picture is now framed on the wall of his Islington home.

- During this exercise, turn off your internal critic, which will inhibit your creativity and natural expression. Think to yourself: 'I can draw no wrong on the page.' Draw anything, anyhow, without thinking about why. Allow yourself total freedom; let the colours flow, and shapes and symbols to form naturally on the paper. You could even draw with your eyes closed. Go with the flow, and let what needs to be expressed emerge on the page. When you have finished, free associate around what you have drawn, without criticism. Often paintings like these provide clues and unexpected connections which can solve problems in our lives.

- A mandala (*see page* 33) represents the universe. It is usually a circle enclosing a square containing a symbol. In psychotherapy, mandalas can be used to express a person's striving for the unity of self: Dr Carl Jung created mandalas repeatedly as his own form of therapy. Design mandalas to express your visions of yourself, and the world. Are the two diagrams similar in any way?

- Draw an advertisement for yourself, expressing all your qualities visually. What do you want others to recognize in you? If you do this exercise in a group, pass the pictures around, so that people can add more positive images and comments to them.

- Draw a pie chart of feelings: decide how much space different feelings occupy in your present life. Use different materials to represent different feelings – inks, crayons, paints and charcoal – and experiment with colours and brush strokes. Are the divisions between the feelings clear, or blurry in some cases?

PRINCIPLES OF ART THERAPIES

- Using pencil, draw an image in black and white of something that distresses you. When you have finished, visualize how you would like the situation to be. Now paint over the original drawing using colours, to change it to how you would like it to be. Focus on the new image. This can be your reality. What action can you take now to begin to effect the change?

- Draw someone you have deeply negative feelings for.

  NB It is important to recognize that the way you see other people may have more to do with the way you see yourself than the way they are. A characteristic you dislike in another person may be a characteristic you dislike in yourself. Bearing this in mind, you could draw the person as a component of a self-portrait, or part of the person as yourself.

  Ensure that you transform the picture to be more positive, by adding light colours, for example.

- Concentrate your thoughts on a person who is important to you. Draw this person, not 'realistically', but as an analogue – a pattern of lines, dots or shapes, or a mixture, that represent the person. Highly abstract shapes or patterns can be instantly recognizable to other people as personality types – and they bypass conventional modes of description.

- Draw a symbol for one of your negative emotions, then draw a symbol for a positive one. Draw a route from the negative one to the positive one. Is the road long or short? Does it follow a straightforward or winding path? Is it precarious and fraught with danger, or flat and easy to negotiate? Draw another route from the new feeling. Where does it lead to?

- Paint a set of symbols: a flame of energy, a sword of strength, a rose of love, a rainbow of passion, and an island of serenity. Think about how and where these can be used in your life. Maybe your flame could help you put more power into creating business contacts – to make that extra call. Visualize this happening, and stick the flame somewhere you are likely to see it regularly, such as in your personal organizer. The symbol of love might help you to make an extra commitment or express more sensitivity. You could cut it out, and deliver it right now!

- Using means–end arrow diagrams (*see page 37*), draw where you have been in your life (include significant milestones), where you are now, and where you would like to be. Use means–end lines to take you there. You can use three separate sheets of paper, or combine the three aspects on one page.

In this exercise, you move from the general to the specific (e.g. from buying a house to writing a new c.v.), so you will need to spend time developing the details.

PRINCIPLES OF ART THERAPIES

MUSIC

What passion cannot music raise and quell?

JOHN DRYDEN

Sitting on the sofa in the doldrums you click on a CD in your stereo: 'Sitting in the morning sun …' You start humming along, your mood changes, and soon you feel better.

If music did not have this effect, it would not be the multi-billion dollar industry that it is. As William Cowper (1731–1800) wrote in his poem 'The Task':

> There is in souls a sympathy with sounds,
> And as the mind is pitched, the ear is pleased
> With melting airs, or martial, brisk, or grave;
> Some chord in unison with what we hear
> Is touched within us, and the heart replies.

Curiously, the effects of music in therapy have not often been studied.

I will always remember the first time I heard Tina Turner singing 'Private Dancer'. I was a struggling adolescent, and suddenly this wrenching sound roared into me, transmitting suffering and strength in an extraordinary way. The music communicated to me a pain that I had not experienced but could nevertheless understand.

When Tina Turner sings 'What's love got to do with it?', you know the feelings are for real, that she means it and that she has triumphed over adversity. 'Better Be Good To Me' was written by Rupert Hine and his girlfriend Jenette Obstoj after Tina had told to them her life story. When she heard the demo tape for the first time, it was so powerful that she wept.

Tina Turner's life is a story of triumph over fear, suffering, pain and torment. Aged forty, she had experienced years of abuse. She had only debts, a job as a cleaner and an absolute iron determination to succeed. This determination powers through the music which has made Tina Turner an international star.

In Ancient China, once a year, in the second month, Emperor Shun journeyed east to check on his kingdom, and ensure that all state affairs were in order in his vast land.

He did not audit the account books of the regions, interview the regional officials, or observe the living conditions of the populace. He believed that music could indicate whether a kingdom was well governed, and if its morals were good or bad. In accordance with Ancient Chinese texts, Emperor Shun listened to musicians playing eight kinds of Chinese musical instruments, and to local folk songs. He measured precisely the pitches of the notes, listened to the crucial five notes of the Ancient Chinese scale, and verified that the music was in perfect correspondence with the five tones.

If Emperor Shun found that neighbouring regions were tuned differently, he would consider it inevitable that they would go to war. If the music was vulgar and coarse, he assumed that immorality would sweep across the nation unless action was taken to correct it.

The Ancient Chinese believed that civilizations were moulded according to the kinds of music performed within them. If the music was romantic, the people would be romantic; if it had a strong, military style, the people would be fearless and forceful. The citizens would remain stable as long as the music remained unchanged; if the style of music altered, however, so would the people's way of life.

The essence of Ancient Chinese music was a tone called the *huang chung*, which means 'yellow bell' – the phrase also refers to both the ruler and divine will. This tone formed the basis of all the systems of the state. Because it was so important, a special pipe of specific dimensions was made to produce it. Its length became the standard Chinese length of measurement, its capacity determined the standard volume, and the number of grains of rice that it contained formed the standard unit of weight.

The philosopher Confucius believed that good music could help to perfect character: 'The music of the noble-minded man is mild and delicate. It keeps a uniform mood, it enlivens and moves.' The Ancient Greeks used music as a curative or preventive: they considered its effects on physical and mental states to be predictable.

The power of music to stir and shape the spirit is expressed in the Greek legend of Orpheus. Orpheus' music was so great that it soothed not only animals, but also plants, rocks and even the elements. When his wife Eurydice died of a snake bite, Orpheus in desperation descended to the Underworld. The great musician played to Hades, ruler of the Underworld, and the beautiful music of his lyre caused Hades to weep tears of iron. Hades offered Orpheus a chance to rescue his wife, on condition that Orpheus did not look back while his wife followed him out of the Underworld. Yet Orpheus had not

PRINCIPLES OF ART THERAPIES

perfected the music in his own spirit, and lacked faith in his wife, for he looked back.

In his book *The Therapeutic Value of Music*, Manly Hall tells the story of how a disturbed young man forced his way into the house of a judge who had recently sentenced his criminal father to death. The frenzied youth, 'bearing a naked sword, approached the judge, who was dining with friends, and threatened his life. Among the guests was a Pythagorean. Reaching over quietly, he struck a chord upon a lyre which had been laid aside by a musician who had been entertaining the gathering. At the sound of the music, the crazed young man stopped in his tracks and could not move. He was led away as though in trance.' This story dramatically illustrates how music can touch you with power that is deep and immediate.

Soldiers in battle have traditionally used music to invigorate them on the battlefield. Armies have always treated their bands as very important, and trumpeters and drummers have proved highly effective in wars. After the early crusaders were defeated by the Saracens, they adopted their opponents' martial tunes, and went on to victory in their warfare.

Few people today would allow the *huang chung* the celestial powers accorded by the Ancient Chinese. But the principles of order, and the power of music to affect our emotions still hold true. Certainly, many people today search for harmony within themselves using music. You know when you are living fluently and in harmony with yourself: your emotions, thoughts, experiences and relationships form graceful, unified patterns. Music can lead you to this state: it heals in the fullest sense, harmonizing all aspects of your being – the physical, emotional, mental and spiritual.

Johann Sebastian Bach studied the music of Vivaldi, in particular 'L'Estro Armonico', in order to refine his own ideas. Vivaldi

organized his concertos into three movements: the two at the   **47**
beginning and end were fast, and the middle one slow, to cap-
ture an emotional theme using a beautiful tone. As Dennis
Arnold comments in his book *Bach*: 'Vivaldi had grasped the
principle of key modulation, that is the home key or tonic, which
represents a resting place while other keys give varying degrees
of discomfort or tension. Thus there is the possibility of contrast-
ing emotions, and perhaps even pastel shades of these emotions.'

HOW MUSIC THERAPY WORKS

Alison is a 24-year-old graphic designer. Whenever she feels
miserable, she turns to music for solace. She used not to know
quite why, and would listen to whatever was at hand. When
she did a music therapy course, she selected music that accorded
with her moods, and compiled tapes that she chooses between
if she feels anxious, depressed or lacking in energy.

What do you enjoy listening to? What would set you buzzing
if your feelings started to drift downwards?

The ability of music to access and alter moods is astounding.
The film director Frederico Fellini once said that he feared
using too much music in his films as it threatened to over-
whelm his words and images and make them redundant.
Music holds and moves our feelings: it arranges changing feelings through time, and stimulates corresponding feelings in the
listeners. Music is something we can share with other people –
it takes us on a journey together.

You can use music to rearrange and compose your mood,
and to orchestrate your feelings so that they supercharge you
throughout the day. Modern technology makes it easy for you
to wake up in the morning to a magnificent concerto, a blast of
rock music, or a jazz freestyle. Yet what do most of us wake up
to? The traffic news on the radio.

48   Music animates emotions on a level below conscious feeling, and can have dramatic effects on your physiology: this is related to the fact that the roots of the auditory nerves are more widely distributed and have more connections than any other nerves in the body. Harmonious (consonant) and discordant (dissonant) chords, and different intervals between notes influence your pulse and respiration; sustained chords lower your blood pressure, and crisp, repeated chords raise it. Generally, muscular energy increases with the intensity and pitch of musical sounds. Harmonious rhythms can, depending on the tempo, be effective sedatives or stimulants: a piece of music with the tempo of a normal heartbeat (60–80 beats per minute) soothes; rhythms which are slower than heartbeat build suspense – it is as though the body anticipates the music will speed up. Fast rhythms raise the heart rate and excite the whole body.

SUITABILITY

Because music connects directly with your feelings, it is especially well suited to working with extreme emotional states. If you feel anxious, you can use music to calm you, then go on to investigate your situation in relaxed manner – which gives you a better chance of a successful outcome.

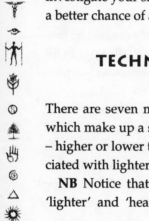

TECHNIQUES USED IN MUSIC

PITCH

There are seven musical notes – Do, Re, Mi, Fa, Sol, La, Ti – which make up a scale. Scales are repeated at different octaves – higher or lower than each other. Usually, high notes are associated with lighter feelings, and lower tones with heavier ones.

NB Notice that in order to describe feelings, I have used 'lighter' and 'heavier' in this instance, whereas elsewhere I images for describing feelings.

MELODY

This is the movement from one note to another over time. In order to be effectively melodic, and not move jarringly from one note to another, there must be continuity in the transition. Emotional transformation needs to happen in a similar way: smoothly, and moving through various stages.

HARMONY

Harmony is several notes played at the same time. Harmony makes the incongruous compatible, achieving order from chaos.

LOUDNESS

Loudness can vary from the crash of a cymbal to the softness of a flute. Louder and softer sounds can express anger or dreaminess, for example.

RHYTHM

The rhythm or beat of a melody is often identified as its key constituent. It imposes unanimity on the divergent: most of the time it remains constant while the notes change. Rhythm creates patterns of expectation because of its consistency, so variations become exciting.

'LET IT BE'

'Let It Be' is a famous song by John Lennon, written when relationships between the Beatles had become strained. John Lennon woke up one morning inspired by a dream in which his mother Mary appeared to him and told him not to worry so much about things – to let them be. He worked the dream into

the celebrated song, which moves from a sad, soulful mood to something more strident.

- The pitch of the music oscillates between higher and lower tones so that the 'let it be' refrain is emotionally uplifting.
- In the melody, one note progresses logically on the next, but sometimes there is a surprise, which is very satisfying.
- When the song digresses from the main harmony, it returns to it at the refrain.
- Loudness powerfully emphasizes the central message of the song.
- Although the rhythm starts off slowly, it speeds up, creating a sense of movement away from the sadder emotions.

SELECTING MUSIC FOR YOURSELF

Instead of listening to music randomly flung through the airwaves by radio stations, or playing consecutive tracks from a tape you have bought, make a collection of music which you can use to change your mood. Here are three suggestions to start you off.

- 'Voices of Spring' by Johann Strauss (Jr) – this has a tremendous rise and rise in optimism and velocity.
- 'Right Through You' by Alanis Morissette – an angry, cathartic song that achieves honest resolution.
- The *Rocky* theme tune – the rhythms express tenacity and evoke a sense of endurance.

Mark is a young man in his twenties with profound learning difficulties. He used to spend his entire day, every day, moving agitatedly backwards and forwards in a repetitive motion. He could not talk, and he never acknowledged the presence of another person, although he would eat when food was placed before him. However, the nursing staff in the residential unit where he lived observed that he did sometimes appear to interact with people, with a distant look in his eyes. Music therapy was used as a way of trying to relate to him.

The therapist began by playing pieces of popular music with strong rhythmic beats, and providing a selection of percussion instruments – tambourine, castanets and bells. Initially Mark continued his rocking movements independently of the musical rhythm. He rejected all the percussion instruments by placing them beside him. As the therapist copied Mark's movements, Mark's rhythm moved more closely in line with the musical beat. Twenty minutes into the second session, he burst into a grin, and started to sing along to the music.

The music therapy sessions continued on a weekly basis. After five sessions, Mark began to clap in time with the music. Later, he used some of the percussion instruments. In the middle of the twelfth session he stood up and began to dance in time to the music. He varied his movements in response to those made by the therapist. One nurse was astonished: it was the most spontaneous activity she had seen him do in seven years.

EXERCISES

Try the following, using tone, pitch, melody, harmony, loudness and rhythm. You do not have to be able to read music or have formally learned to play an instrument for any of the exercises. You can even use home-made instruments, such as yoghurt pots with dried peas, milk bottles with different levels of water, jam jars and metal tins.

- Make music which is close to and far from your current emotional state, then make a bridge between them. For example, if you feel sad, make sad sounds, then happy sounds, and experiment with ways of getting from one to the other. Use pure tones as well as chords and tunes. Listening to simple sounds can help you to concentrate on the key mood conveyed to you.

- Do you associate particular pieces of music with certain events? Select pieces of music that accord with feelings you have had at certain times of your life.

- Make a list of simple tunes that you associate with anger, sadness and fear. Sing them in your head. Experiment with moving between one song and another, and using them to shift your emotional state.

- Sing different tones to change your emotional state. You might start with a low tone, and then move higher, or try the opposite. How does this affect your feelings? What tones do you associate with illness, health, success and laughter?

- Play different types of music: loud, soft, rapid and harmonious. What life events do you recall when you play each type?

- Create a set of energy sounds. What chord or tone would you like to associate with confidence, power, energy and calm? Inject your mind with a drumbeat, or a triangle sound, to make you feel confident, or calm, for example.

- Choose a chore that you do frequently and do not particularly enjoy, such as cleaning the house, doing homework, or revising accounts. Perform it to three kinds of music: rock, waltz and piano. How do your experiences vary?

    NB At the end of this exercise, you may have achieved something that you have put off for a while.

- Focus on yourself as an instrument for sound. This exercise is a lot of fun, but you need to cast off all your inhibitions! Move to the different sounds you make, if you are working in a group, one person can make the sounds and the others can explore moving to them, or pair up with someone else, and bounce the sounds between you.

    Try the following: 'grrrrrrrrrrr', 'buzzzzzzzzzz', 'ooooooooh', 'haaaaaaaaaa' and 'mmmmmmmmmmmmm'. Then combine them: 'yeeeeeeeeeehaaaaaaa', 'oooooooompaaaaaaah', 'ooooooooooyeeeeeeeeah'.

- Standing or sitting, close your eyes. Breathe in and out three times. Let your body move and sway a little to ensure that you are not holding yourself too tightly. Focus your mind on your breathing. Let your body and breathing become smooth, to smooth out any knots. Notice the smoothness of your breathing, as the air flows cleanly into your lungs without effort. Feel your whole body become calm and smooth. Now open your mouth a little, and make a sound as you exhale, with the least possible effort. Continue to focus your attention on your breathing and your body. Don't strain to make the sound, just let it flow naturally out of you. If you are doing this as a group exercise, the sound will come together as one smooth chant, which can be very restful. Notice the changes in rise and fall of volume and pitch.

Music, said the bard:

Can minister to minds diseased
Pluck from the memory a rooted sorrow
Raze out the written troubles of the brain
And with its sweet, oblivious antidote
Cleanse the full bosom of all perilous stuff
Which weighs upon the heart.

DRAMA

> If you create an act, you create a habit. If you create a habit,
> you create a character. If you create a character, you create
> a destiny.
>
> ANDRÉ MAUROIS

'Doctor, are you prescribing me a course of twelve sessions of
EastEnders?'

'Yes.'

Well, it's not a very likely scenario, I agree. But it does closely
model the attitude of the Ancient Greeks, who used drama as
medicine. At Epidaurus, the theatre was attached to a healing
centre, which was used for treating both spiritual and physical
ailments.

When you see a great piece of drama, be it Shakespeare's
A Midsummer Night's Dream or George Lucas' *Star Wars*, you
don't only enjoy the action, you leave the auditorium changed.
You walk out feeling different about yourself, your life and
other people. That is why you go.

Pain and suffering in drama can heal you emotionally, and
help you to progress to greater levels of understanding of yourself and empathy with others.

THE ORIGINS OF DRAMA

Dionysus is the Greek god of wine, fruitfulness and vegetation. He is also the bestower of ecstasy and god of drama, and in Ancient Greece, he was worshipped in orgiastic rites. The dancers and singers wore costumes and masks to represent the characters, and at revels, their faces were smothered in the deep purple dregs of wine.

In Athens, citizens had a duty to attend the theatre: tickets were provided out of public funds. Theatre had a purpose other than entertainment: it was where issues of public morality were debated, and it was a form of public education. Both comedies and tragedies were performed.

HOW DRAMA WORKS

In the theatre, illusion and reality coincide. Acting involves outwardly imitating appearance and movement, and inwardly adopting a character: every character on the stage is a symbol of reality.

The actor uses symbols of reality, in the same way that a poet uses images and metaphors: he selects gestures, tones and movements that balance the actual and the imaginary. The great actress Eleonora Duse (1858–1924) insisted that a bowl of real flowers always be present on her stage. She used this graceful symbol as her symbol of reality in the imaginary world being presented on the stage.

The actor's art is based on two elements: acting techniques, which he uses to mask his character and assume another; and a poised, dignified presence on stage.

There are two cornerstones of acting theory.

1) Presentational acting – the actor imitates speech, movements, mannerisms and emotions. While the actor *may* feel the emotions, the main task during performance is to adhere to a series of carefully constructed actions which convey the concept of the character.

2) Method acting – the actor attempts to actually think the thoughts and feel the feelings of the character portrayed, by drawing on his own experiences. He believes that every moment on stage must be in line with the inner life of the character.

Constantin Stanislavski (1863–1938), founder of the Moscow Art Theatre, observed that great actors can step into the imaginary situation of a play, so that the events on stage seem to them actually to be happening. The spectator is filled with a deep sense of belief in the character and her behaviour. These actors use both presentational and method techniques of acting – mastery of the voice and body, a thorough understanding of the character's psychology, and an ability to evoke emotions that ring true because they are derived from the actors' personal experiences.

In the theatre, life is exaggerated. Everything becomes unusually important, and every action must be justified. Often actions happen for reasons which are far-fetched and would be considered unlikely or even absurd in everyday life. But the actor must believe it completely, otherwise he will resort to clichés. The actor unravels the meaning of the action and discovers rhythm in the seemingly incoherent unfolding of events.

Constantin Stanislavski used acting as a way of explaining the human personality. By adopting different roles, he found he could better understand himself. This principle was adopted by Joseph Moreno, who worked with a form of drama therapy which he called psychodrama.

Because the actor is imagining a situation, in some ways he has greater emotional freedom to react to it. He can release himself to the deepest emotions of grief or terror, knowing that after the performance, he can distance himself from those feelings and everything will be alright. So, paradoxically, because theatre is not 'reality', it is a safer place to express emotions than real life. Because of this, the emotions expressed on stage are often more authentic than those we usually express in everyday life. John, an actor in his forties, sees one of the prime purposes of his work as releasing his audience from their own barriers, to allow them to feel emotions that they normally suppress.

Transference is a term used in psychology to describe how we direct our attitudes and emotions away from ourselves, towards a substitute. The spectator of a drama directs his emotions towards the actors rather than towards himself. The actor is a symbol of reality on the stage, with which the spectator becomes emotionally involved.

In drama therapy, the imagined worst – the past trauma you were afraid to face up to, or the emotion you were avoiding – can be met and survived. In present-day situations, we often subconsciously react to situations in ways we would have reacted years ago, but which are no longer appropriate. If you consciously act out past events, you face up to them, and become aware of your behaviour: only when you are aware of your behaviour can you begin to change it.

Drama gives you an opportunity to think differently about yourself. It takes you into new situations and roles, and so becomes a new way of exploring life, values and relationships. You can enter situations on an 'as if' basis; you can emulate new roles, find different ways of doing things, and alter entrenched, ineffective patterns of behaviour very quickly.

Taking on the roles of other characters gives you the opportunity to break down your character armour. By choosing a different posture, using different language and behaviour, you gain control over your own actions and behaviour, and increase your ability to relate to people who are different from you. Moreno used these techniques to help people empathize with others. Ultimately, we all want to reach out and connect with other people: it is a fundamental need.

Many great actors prepare for their roles by engaging beforehand in the emotional state which they are about to perform. Thus an actor about to display anger will work himself up into a rage in the wings of the theatre before walking on stage.

You could use the same technique to prepare yourself for an interview, for example, when you need to be bright, positive and radiating energy. I spent some time working with the long-term unemployed. When we did mock interviews, I discovered that people with fantastic, relevant, life and work experience for a job would present themselves with such a lack of energy that there was no way they would get the job. By 'revving up' before interview, they got themselves into a more energetic frame of mind. Happily, many of the people working in these groups successfully obtained the jobs they wanted.

PRINCIPLES OF ART THERAPIES

DRAMA AND UNDERSTANDING

The television and film series *Star Trek* influences a vast number of people across the world. When actor Patrick Stewart took on the role of Captain Jean-Luc Picard in the second *New Generation* series, it took him a while to realize that he had not simply taken on a role – he had assumed a cultural responsibility. Yet *Star Trek* is not even about our world.

In his book *The Making of Star Trek*, creator Gene Rodenberry commented on the Horta, a rock-eating lava monster that featured in the episode 'The Devil in the Dark': 'The Horta was an underground creature which attacked a group of miners. In the end they find out that it attacked because – surprise – it was a mother! It was protecting its eggs because the miners were destroying them in the belief that they were just strange-looking mineral formations. With this understood, the Horta suddenly became understandable too. It wasn't just a monster – it was someone. And the audience could put themselves in the place of the Horta ... identify ... feel! That's what drama is all about. If you can learn to feel for a Horta, you may also be learning to understand and feel for humans of different colours, ways and beliefs.'

SUITABILITY

Drama is well suited for exploring relationships with other people, and feelings you are avoiding. It allows you to identify and empathize with others and examine how you project and internalize your feelings.

Children are brilliant at evoking and playing with imaginary situations. They have not yet learned the 'correct' social responses and conventions that adults use to conceal their true feelings. When children are not cynical or inhibited, they react as unique individuals with great freshness.

'Caught in the Act' are a group of actors employed by the Theatre in Health Education charity. They work with over 30,000 children every year, using drama as a means to communicate. The theatre company believes that the power of role play is very effective, and that once children have overcome a fear in an 'as if' situation, they can much more easily conquer obstacles in reality.

EMOTION MEMORY

Stanislavski coined this term. It is the technique of recollecting an event that you have experienced in real life, in order to portray a similar experience on stage. When Cleopatra bemoans the absence of Anthony, the actress using emotion memory invokes the emotions by recalling her own feelings of frustration while going out with an indecisive man. These are the emotions she will express in the theatre.

Everyone experiences emotion memory. If you tell a friend about being angry with a lover, you might start to repeat what you were saying to him. Your anger increases as you recall the situation – and all of a sudden you are really annoyed.

EXERCISE

To experience emotion memory, think of a time of great joy in your life. Even if it was a very long time ago, you need only recall one detail, and you will discover that one memory leads

on to another. Don't focus on how you feel, but on giving an objective description of the surroundings. Are you indoors or outdoors? In a big room, or a small room? Is it light or dark? Are you alone or with other people? If there are people around you, how many are there? Who are they? What are they wearing? What are they doing?

Recollecting the event may not evoke the identical emotion – as the Greek philosopher Heraclitus said: 'You can only step in the same river once,' for the next time the waters have moved on – but it can be very similar.

TECHNIQUES USED IN DRAMA

ACTION

A physical action can be precisely defined and duplicated, unlike an emotion, which constantly changes in intensity and moves in ways you do not expect. Imitation is a core art of the actor – who need not passively hope for the right feeling to come along: when he performs specific actions with full conviction, the feelings flow of their own accord.

This shows that by taking control of your physical actions, you can help to regulate your emotions. You cannot control emotions, but sometimes you can control what produces them.

PLOT

This is the arrangement of incidents in a drama to achieve a unified whole.

CHARACTER

This is the combination of traits and qualities which distinguish the individual nature of a person, and which reveal personal choice. The qualities portrayed in a drama should be vivid and lifelike.

The arrangement of the lines and speeches must be clear, and the use of words expressive.

STAGE EFFECTS

These can be simple or sophisticated. Their purpose is to enhance the atmosphere of the drama and create a spectacle.

'JEZEBEL'

It is often said that most of our communication is non-verbal. But how often do we take advantage of this information? Bette Davis adopted the principles of the French elocutionist and drama teacher François Delsarte who taught that: 'Every movement is the manifestation of a thought, an emotion, a passion.' In her biography of Bette Davis, Barbara Leaming describes how the actress used her whole body while acting. In the film *Jezebel*, Bette changes physically: powerful emotions slowly and visibly surge in a wavelike movement passing from one part of her body to another.

SELECTING DRAMA FOR YOURSELF

Instead of watching any old film on the television, or going to a cinema to see a film just because it is showing, select a film on the basis of how you are feeling, and how you wish to feel. Compose a list of films and plays that change your emotional state, then explore how they achieve this. Here are some suggestions.

- *It's a Wonderful Life*, directed by Frank Capra – a heartwarming film that tackles darkness and despair, with a movement from despondency to optimism.

- *A Midsummer Night's Dream*, by William Shakespeare – inconsistent pathways to love.
- *Baghdad Café*, directed by Percy Adlon – explores an unexpected personal transformation and harmony reached through traumatic events.
- *The Shawshank Redemption*, written and directed by Frank Darabont – 'Fear can hold you prisoner. Hope can set you free.'
- *A Matter of Life and Death*, directed by Powell and Pressburger – love triumphs over everything – provided you believe.
- *When Harry Met Sally*, directed by Rob Reiner – will jolt your understanding about relationships with members of the opposite sex.

CASE STUDIES

Connie attended a weekly psychodrama group. Her daughter had tragically been killed four years earlier in a car accident, and her relationship with her husband had floundered ever since. She had never faced her feelings around her bereavement: she felt numb. In psychodrama sessions, Connie relived the trauma with the support of other group members, and was able to share her experiences with them. Having faced up to her emotions, she moved on to rehearse and reframe some of the destructive patterns in her relationship with her husband. At the end of two courses of eight psychodrama sessions, Connie and her husband were beginning to talk with each other about their grief, and their relationship was improving.

Broadmoor Psychiatric Hospital in England is a unit for the most disturbed criminal members of society – people who have transgressed its moral and social boundaries. In May 1991, members of the Royal Shakespeare Company, the Royal National Theatre and the Wilde Theatre Company performed a series of Shakespeare plays to patients there.

Actor Mark Rylance played Hamlet and Romeo. It seemed to him that 'the line between reality and fantasy was much more fluid than normal' – as though the play was 'real' to the patients. One of the doctors was sitting with three of her patients while watching *Romeo and Juliet*. One of the patients had killed a man when he had taken some shoes back to a shop, because the shopkeeper had refused to give his money back. After the performance they discussed the feelings that the play had evoked. The psychiatrist told Mark Rylance: 'You have done in a moment what couldn't have been done in years of therapy. I couldn't have spoken so directly to them and shown them the outcome of temper.'

EXERCISES

Drama has particular power when done in a group. Whilst it is not necessary to work with others, it is far more effective than if you do it alone. I would encourage you to experiment with doing some of the exercises with other people. When working with others, you cannot cruise through your carefully planned actions as you can when you are alone: you must contend with their goals and aims. You must adapt, give and take. Try the following exercises, using the techniques of action, plot, character, diction, thought, spectacle and music.

- Focus on a time when you were the happiest you have ever been. How did you behave? Recapture that state, firstly by recalling where you were at the time, and the details of your surroundings. Move on to recall who you were with and what you were doing. When you have recaptured the

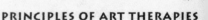

PRINCIPLES OF ART THERAPIES

feeling of happiness, think of a symbol that you can use to represent it: an object in the outside world, something in your imagination, or a combination of the two.

- Perform the same actions in different ways. For example, walk or dance wildly, sadly and hopefully. Imagine yourself standing on the seashore, waving your arm as a sign to the boat carrying your smuggler friends that it is safe for them to return to shore. Now wave to an ex-girlfriend who you notice on the other side of a busy shopping centre. How do the actions differ?

- This exercise will help you to feel bright and energetic when you wake up.

    Lie on your bed, and act how you feel when you first awaken. Leap up into a standing position and shout 'Wake up!' with as much energy, passion, humour and enthusiasm as you can. (Watch out you don't smash into lights, etc.) Repeat this five times. Please try it – it can be very effective. The next time you wake up, you will have reconditioned yourself to start your day with a spring.

- To become more aware of how you express yourself physically, observe yourself in the mirror communicating fear, love, hate and inspiration. Now express a feeling that is outside your normal range. How about being astounded? What gestures do you make when you feel this way? What facial expressions do you make? When did you last feel this way? Isn't it astounding to be alive?

- Act out how situations with friends, parents and enemies appear to you. Now act out the same situation from the other person's perspective, to help you understand the motivations and feelings behind their behaviour.

- Say out loud the same statement, issue or idea, focusing on each of the following in turn:

1) passion
2) sincerity
3) energy.

It is often better to practise with a neutral phrase like 'The rain in Spain falls mainly on the plain', to help you focus on the way you communicate, rather than what you are saying.

How do you feel different each time? Are you making the impression you desire with the clarity you intend? Ask for feedback from the rest of the group.

- Observe how you empathize with others, using body posture and movement. In pairs, try matching each other's movements. Observe the effect on how you feel, and your partner's reaction to you. Does this offer you an opportunity to enhance and deepen your relationships?

- Think of something that you would like to do, but don't believe you can. Focus on it in your mind, and act as if you could do it: stand how you would stand, breathe the way you would breathe, and adjust your posture to how it would be if you did this thing. Now act out doing it.

  The power of action is such that by this point, people often feel that they can do things they had previously considered impossible. Then they DO them! By imitating confidence, it becomes real, and this opens up the possibility of action.

- Think about your shadow roles – the darker, nastier sides of yourself. Act out some examples, then act out your bright 'flare' roles. Where do you feel you are now in relation to these two elements of your psyche? How could you be closer to the bright flare side? What stops you being this way right now? Decide immediately to take on this role!

- Use your senses to exercise your imagination. Work through each of the five senses, one at a time. Recall a place you have visited, such as a wood or a beach. Describe out loud everything that you saw, all the smells and tastes you experienced, everything you heard, and everything you would feel if you were to handle all the imaginary objects around you.

  Next, consider one taste, smell, touch or sound you adore, and one you abhor. What effect do they have on you? How would you show others the effect they have on you?

- Practise conceiving and believing an imaginary situation. Pack an imaginary wardrobe into an imaginary suitcase. In your mind's eye, you are leaving home and divorcing your husband. See the size of each dress, feel its weight and texture.

  Now pack the case for a different reason. This time, you are attending a prestigious international fashion show in Japan. How do your actions differ?

- Imagine your employee is coming to your home for dinner. How do you prepare? Are you laying on a casual or a formal meal? Do you leave the living room in a mess or do you try to create an impression by leaving beautiful books on the coffee table?

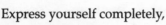

Express yourself completely,
then keep quiet.
Be like the forces of nature:
when it blows there is only wind; when it showers,
  there is only rain;
when the clouds pass, the sun shines through.

FROM *TAO TE CHING* BY LAO-TZU

PRINCIPLES OF ART THERAPIES

POETRY

When power leads man towards arrogance, poetry reminds him of his limitations. When power narrows the areas of man's concern, poetry reminds him of the richness and diversity of his existence. When power corrupts, poetry cleanses. For art establishes the basic human truths which must serve as the touchstone of our judgement.

JOHN F. KENNEDY

It started out as a bright sunny morning. The staff and residents of the home were optimistic, but by early evening, tempers were severely frayed. We were in a large minibus on a 12 hour trip from Clapton in London to Pwythelli in Wales. After seven hours of travelling, we discovered that we had taken a wrong turn, without noticing, some three hours earlier. Everyone was angry. Mike, who was prone to severe mood swings and emotional outbursts, stood up and began to swear in the back of the bus. Gradually, his displays increased in volume and intensity. We had hours' of travelling to go. Mike was stamping his foot and banging on the window of the minibus. It rapidly became unbearable. We asked him to be quiet, but he hammered louder and more frequently, and started shouting obscenities. We tried using behaviour therapy techniques, cognitive techniques, and psychodynamic methods to calm him down. None of them worked. One resident told him forcefully to shut up, and Mike smashed his fist into the side of the bus. It was getting dark outside, and everyone was exhausted. A colleague had the great idea that I should sit next to Mike, to calm him down. Reluctantly I did so, but Mike only became more agitated. I tried to escape the situation by reading some poems by Shelley amid the din of banging. After a short while, Mike asked if he could read the book. I gave it to him unenthusiastically, and he read a poem out loud. I can still remember the thundering power of the words as he read 'To Jane':

> Her voice did quiver as we parted.
> Yet knew I not that heart was broken
> From which it came and I departed
> Heeding not the words then spoken.
> Misery – O Misery.
> This world is all too wide for thee.

After Mike read the poem, an incredible calm descended upon the bus. He became quiet and relaxed, and the journey proceeded peacefully.

The reading of the poem had the power to transform an emotional state in an extraordinary and powerful way.

Some time ago, I did a phone-in for London Talk Radio on the therapeutic use of poetry. Callers told how poetry had helped them overcome problems as diverse as drug addiction, unhappy relationships, and child abuse. One caller had started writing poetry aged 14 after the death of her grandmother, when she felt an instinctive need to console herself. Another caller described how she wrote about her drugs problem which had started at an early age. She conquered her addiction, but other problems followed: her daughter was abused, and she found herself unable to relate to anyone. She sat down one night and suddenly discovered what she had been repressing: 'I didn't know I'd written it and when I came to the end of the page, I read it back, and it was the most horrendous thing to see how I really felt.' She described this as the first step on her recovery.

In a recent article published in *The Lancet*, Dr Robin Phillip analysed the 'spontaneously reported health benefits of poetry in 196 people in the general population'. Forty-two per cent reported that they found the rhythm of poetry helped them, together with identifying with the themes. Fifty-six per cent benefited from writing poetry as an outlet for their emotions. The benefits included reduced stress, better mood, reduced pain during bereavement, reduced physical pain, and coming off antidepressive medication or tranquillizers.

HOW POETRY THERAPY WORKS

In their book *Affect, Cognition and Change*, distinguished clinical and cognitive psychologists John Teasdale and Philip Barnard assert that a poem can communicate a holistic meaning that cannot be conveyed by prose. The impact of a poem depends on the integrated effect of the statements, the sounds of the words, rhymes and meters, and the visual imagery evoked. They give an example from the Keats poem 'La Belle Dame sans Merci':

> O what can ail thee, knight at arms,
> Alone and palely loitering?
> The sedge has withered from the lake,
> And no birds sing.

Teasdale and Barnard provide a literal transcription of the poem, without the sound and visual imagery:

> What is the matter, armed old-fashioned soldier,
> Standing by yourself and doing nothing with a pallid expression?
> The reed-like plants have decomposed by the lake,
> And there are not any birds singing.

Comparing the two versions illustrates how creative art forms can communicate levels of meaning over and above the literal ones.

Aldous Huxley said: 'Words form the thread on which we string our experiences.' Writing a poem can help you attain a new perspective, a sense of control and understanding. Through poetry, you can explore symbols in your mind, free the imagination, evoke emotions and link them with new images and ways of reasoning. You can use it to develop conscious strategies for handling emotions. The rhythms of the words can shape emotions, often by putting the reader into a semi-hypnotic state. The language of poetry is memorable and consequently rapidly accessible and retrievable.

SUITABILITY

In poetry, you can focus very closely on a particular thought, feeling, incident or person. Accurate combinations of words help you to zoom in on an issue. Short poems can be memorized – metaphorically, they can be easily and rapidly digested, so that the effects of their images in the mind are long-lasting.

Writing poetry develops your ability to focus and be precise, and enhances your capacity to generate images.

TECHNIQUES USED IN POETRY

IMAGERY

This is figurative or descriptive language, which expresses ideas economically and which other people can easily relate to.

RHYME

This is a superb technique for locking phrases into the memory: if you believe it and conceive it, you will achieve it.

RHYTHM

This can lead the mind to a hypnotic state. In a lecture on hypnosis at the Royal Society of Medicine, one of the speakers discussed the trance-like state that can be attained while reading or listening to poetry. He described his difficulty in explaining this state to a poet friend of his. 'Don't worry, I understand,' said the poet. 'You mean simply that the poet's wings brushed the air.'

LANGUAGE

Choosing exactly the right words is a great skill. Using precise language is not only useful for defining feelings, but also for re-aligning the emotional world you live in.

A SONNET

This sonnet by William Shakespeare demonstrates the techniques discussed above:

> When in disgrace with fortune and men's eyes
> I all alone beweep my outcast state
> And trouble deaf heaven with my bootless cries
> And look upon myself and curse my fate,
> Wishing myself like one more rich in hope

Featured like him, like him with friends possessed,
Desiring this man's art and that man's scope
With what I most enjoy contented least;
Yet in these thoughts myself almost despising –
Haply I think on thee, and then my state,
Like to the Lark at break of day arising
From sullen earth sings hymns at Heaven's gate;
For thy sweet love remembered such wealth brings
That then I scorn to change my state with kings.

- The poem makes use of the strong image (visual and aural) of the singing lark in the morning.
- Rhymes flow easily and naturally and make the poem memorable.
- The rhythm is steady, then it speeds up at the end of the poem, moving from a solemn to a lighter, more assertive rhythm.
- The language is precise and clearly expresses the changing mood of the poem.

WRITING YOUR OWN POETRY

With poetry, the aim is to focus on the form and the inter-relationships of the words. If writing a story is like building a house, then creating a poem is like concentrating with great care on the individual bricks: their alignment, shape and texture.

If you have not written poetry before, start with free asso-ciation: simply write down whatever enters your head, without judgement. Then, when you have written down some thoughts, feelings and images, you can arrange them into a poem. The exercises at the end of the chapter contain ideas and strategies to help you with this.

Shelley emphasized how important it was to him to gain life experience in order to develop his poetry:

> I have trodden the glaciers of the Alps, and lived under the eye of Mont Blanc. I have been a wanderer among distant fields. I have sailed down mighty rivers, and seen the sun rise and set, and the stars come forth, whilst I have sailed day and night down a rapid stream among mountains. I have seen populous cities, and have watched the passions which rise and spread, and sink and change amongst assembled multitudes of men.

What might you do to bring fresh insights and references into your life? How about a walk by a river, visiting a park, or finding a spot where you can look at the stars.

SELECTING POEMS FOR YOURSELF

By focusing on the images in poems and how you relate to them, you can notice mood changes in poems. Think about the following examples:

- 'Death Be Not Proud', by John Donne – strengthening and courageous.
- 'If thou must love me, let it be for nought', a sonnet by Elizabeth Barrett Browning – an eloquent request for true love.
- 'If', by Rudyard Kipling – sound advice about living.
- 'Upon Westminster Bridge', by William Wordsworth – a cityscape is magically transformed into a place of grace.

CASE STUDIES

Jethro is a manager for an industrial company in his mid-fifties. When he was due to go on holiday, his mother was taken ill, and he didn't know what to do. Working with his therapist, he wrote a poem which helped him to separate the strands that were confused in his mind: worry, guilt, fear and anger conflicted with the desire to go on holiday. Once he had written the poem, Jethro felt better and more congruent in himself. Having determined that the illness was not life-threatening, he resolved firmly to go on holiday.

Myra Schneider is a writer and therapist who uses poems and stories to explore her own life, and to help her clients explore theirs. With John Killick, she wrote *Writing for Self Discovery*. She wrote the poem below after the death of her father, to support her, and provide a way of thinking about a terrible situation that made it more bearable.

LEAVE TAKING

And when he was struck speechless
then I wanted him to speak again
when he couldn't deliver the orders
I wanted to cram back into his mouth,
break the unbearable waters
of wrath over my head
then I wanted to hear his voice again,
would have held out cupped hands
for a command, a judgement, a complaint.

When he was sentenced
to a wordless struggle for breath

and could no longer devour us
with: 'I'm dying: I wish I was dead,'
I discovered what I'd guessed:
he'd cried wolf instead of pain,
stalked by implacable terrors
he dared not name. But he'd given
doctors instructions to haul him
back for the last mile, last inch

to keep tabs on the world,
its disgraced conduct of itself,
his daughter's failings, successes
and the complex finances in his head.
Minutes before his lungs
finally rebelled
his fingers plotted in the air
the upward curve of his grandson's career.

And in those four speechless days
when his eyes fixed
on the precise saline drip
drip thorough glass arteries,
where his hands washed themselves
of the universe or clutching at a pen
produced strange new writing,
did a kind of acceptance trickle through?

In those four speechless days
I began to strip him of shortcomings,
bury the terrible damages
and I hung onto his zest,
and his generosities, his ever-
enquiring scientific mind,

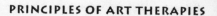

his hunger for consciousness,
that miracle each person carries,
a delicate globe lit
by intricate, unseen filaments
which is so suddenly put out,
which is totally
irreplaceable.

© *Myra Schneider*

EXERCISES

The following exercises involve using imagery, rhyme, rhythm, language and assonance.

- Choose a person, and free associate around them: write down whatever comes into your head when you think of them, no matter how absurd it seems. Next, focus on the words you have used, and arrange them into a poem. Explore how the words you have chosen relate to the ideas and feelings you intend to communicate. What does this person mean to you?

- Create metaphors by asking unexpected questions about everyday objects, feelings and ideas. For example: what colour would sadness be? What coat would it wear? What sort of river would express you? Would it be deep or shallow, windy or straight? Next, structure your answers into a poem. By finding interesting or humorous angles on unpleasant things, you can reframe them and gain some control over them.

    Pablo Neruda was a master of the metaphor, who conjured up unexpected realities with his beautiful words. Instead of saying that he felt low in the afternoon, he wrote:

'Leaning into the afternoon I cast my sad nets towards your oceanic eyes.'

- Select five positive emotions and five negative ones, and write poems about each, keeping them the same length – I suggest 12 lines per poem. Ensure that:

    – each poem has a central image that you can lock into your mind;

    – every negative emotion transmutes into a positive one by the end of the poem. You may find this difficult at first, but this exercise is not about wallowing in despondency. If the emotion you choose is misery, and you use darkness as an image, what is the light at the end of the tunnel, or the torch in the cave?

    When you have written the 10 poems, don't stop there. Explore a state you don't often experience and would like to experience more often: being intrepid, say. The more time you spend investigating a state, the more you are likely to experience it.

- Write some very quick poems – not more than five minutes each – on the past, present, and future, and wishes realized and unrealized. You might be surprised at what emerges.

- Think about what is great about you, even if you do not have an optimistic sense of yourself at present. (Focusing on the negative can create a vicious circle that spirals downwards. Concentrating on the positive can generate an upwards virtuous circle.) Think of a single word that describes you, then free associate, and write words in clusters around your focus word. Then assemble the words into a poem. *(See diagram overleaf.)*

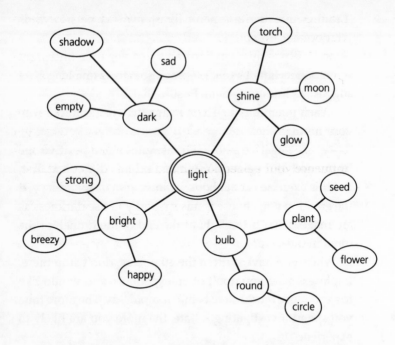

- The act of focusing on positive feelings becomes a way of reinforcing and enhancing them. Focus on the happiness in your life. What gives you this joy? Find a symbol for this feeling, and write a poem that locks it into your mind. Is joy 'the oar that steers you in life's tide', or 'a rose of love that blooms within your soul', for example?

- Choose a sad emotion. Write images, words and phrases that you associate with this feeling. Then devise a way to transform it. With poetry, you have every tool available that you could possibly imagine – quite literally. If shifting a heavy feeling of despair would take all the energy of a national power station – you've got it!

- Write two poems of five lines each, side by side, about a relationship you are in, or have been in. One poem is your view of the relationship, the other is your partner's. Under

PRINCIPLES OF ART THERAPIES

these poems, write a seven line poem about how these
views meet, do not meet and could meet.
- John D. Rockefeller wrote out his credo as a list of 10 statements of belief. His language is so accurate and concise that it approximates a poem.

    Write a list of your 10 fundamental beliefs. Make them into a poem that you are truly proud of, that you can pin on your wall. This powerful statement about yourself will influence your perceptions of and actions in the world.

You can succeed. Go on. You do know how.
There is a way. You have it in you now!

STORIES

It is the function of art to renew our perception. What we are familiar with we cease to see. The writer shakes up the familiar scene, and as if by magic, we see a new meaning in it.

ANAÏS NIN

A poor father and his son owned a small farm. They had a few vegetable plots, some chickens and one marvellous thoroughbred horse. One day the horse ran away.

'How terrible, what bad luck,' said the neighbours.

'Good luck, bad luck, who knows?' replied the farmer.

Several weeks later, the horse returned, bringing in tow five beautiful wild mares.

'What marvellous luck,' said the neighbours.

'Good luck, bad luck, who knows?' said the farmer.

The son trained and learned to ride the horses expertly. But one day he was thrown off one of them and he broke his leg.

'What bad luck,' said the neighbours.

'Good luck, bad luck, who knows?' said the farmer.

The next week the army came to the village to take away all the young men to war. The farmer's son was still disabled with his broken leg. So he could not be recruited.

Good luck, bad luck. Who knows?

This well-known story illustrates the theme of uncertainty, and how we can choose to handle it in different ways.

HOW STORY THERAPY WORKS

Great stories, whether fact or fiction, can change the way you think about your life. You read an epic tale and see how countless strivings, agonies, loves, hopes, passions, despairs and victories belong to one great pattern. Our lives are part of that pattern: you realize that you belong to a wider community that includes the greatest of human heroes. Writer John Irving takes life as it is, and develops its coherence, wonder and fun. In his books, life makes more sense: even pain and awfulness has its place and can be made sense of: he takes terrible themes and fashions them into something bearable and good.

Stories are a great way of making sense of things. Jesus was a brilliant communicator because of his use of parables. He spoke of complex ideas using metaphors that his audience could easily relate to.

Stories provide a different set of references with which you associate your thoughts and feelings, and powerful emotional templates – ways of setting and viewing the world. If you have a negative template, you see the world as an awful place. If you fail an exam, the template says: 'Oh no, here I go again! What a terrible failure I am! What a loser!' A positive template helps you to see what you have gained from the experience. It might say: 'Okay, I didn't pass the exam, but I learned a great lesson about not being anxious, so I'll do better next time.'

Must a relationship ending be only a dreadful, harrowing event? 'When the feeling's gone and you can't go on, tragedy!' sing the BeeGees, yet Gloria Gaynor sings: 'I will survive!'

Your way of seeing the world is self-fulfilling: if you see the world as your enemy, you select examples from your experience which prove this to be the case; if you see the world more positively, you select references which enforce this viewpoint, and your vision becomes true. So, in order to maximize your happiness and achievement, you must build a positive, resilient template. Stories, paintings, poems and music can be used to build up the most wonderful templates that help you to master your emotions and take control of your life.

The psychiatrist Bruno Bettelheim describes in his book *The Uses of Enchantment* how in Hindu medicine people are traditionally told fairy tales in order to help them overcome psychological disturbances. Fairy tales have great transformational power. The stories are enjoyable because of their wonderful use of symbols: a rose is not merely a rose – it becomes a symbol of love, sexuality, hope or doom. Lessons are taught with symbols. So, for example: a strong white horse must be killed – the wild recklessness that led the boy through his youth must be sacrificed to make way for his adult achievements and responsibilities.

Here is an example of how different versions of the same story can influence the way you see the world. Imagine that you read the following article about a new pharmaceutical Clearzine in a respectable medical journal:

In a random study of 175 patients, Clearzine reduced anxiety within 48 hours to normal levels for 98 per cent of the sample, and provided relief from the symptoms of clinical depression for 68 per cent of the sample. No side effects have been detected in any instance.

The set of beliefs you construct may differ if a stallholder at your local market says:

'Feeling jittery? Slip one of these tablets in your tea to calm you down. Always works, I promise.'

SUITABILITY

Writing and reading stories is most suitable for addressing problems which require big, long-term changes. They can also help you to prepare for setbacks in reality. By showing characters handling setbacks, stories can prevent you from despairing, and carry you through with the belief that it is possible to overcome obstacles and go on to a successful outcome. Stories demonstrate possibilities, through fact or fiction.

The celebrated story of Roger Banister is an excellent example. Until he cracked the four minute mile, no one believed it was possible. Afterwards, everyone was doing it: they knew it was possible, so it became an achievable goal. Pretty soon, running the mile in under four minutes became commonplace. Yet all the runners had to go on was the story in their minds that it had been done. That set the template and helped them to construct a pattern of aims and possibilities.

TECHNIQUES USED IN STORY-WRITING

PLOT

This is how what moves events on and connects them. It parallels how we divide up our life experiences. Is the plot of your life full of isolation and misunderstanding? Or does a bright end come into view after setbacks?

One man with political ambitions failed in business aged 31; lost a legislative race a year later; failed in business again two years later; suffered the death of his lover; had a nervous breakdown; lost another election, three congressional races and two senatorial races. Aged 60, Abraham Lincoln became President of the United States of America.

Stories show cycles and patterns of behaviour through their characters. A positive or negative outcome conveys a message about the efficacy of the patterns.

CHARACTERIZATION

Character defines story. When a character is clearly defined, the narrative flows of its own accord. So it is, I believe, with life. If you truly know yourself, and what you want, your life will follow the pattern of your desires.

SYMBOLS

Symbols are used in stories to connect deeply with the emotions.

A STORY

The following story uses plot, characters, and symbols.

Cronus lusted after the nymph Philyra and pursued her to the town of Thessaly. Philyra transformed herself into a mare to escape him, but he changed himself into a stallion, and copulated with her.

This was how Chiron the Centaur came to be. In Greek myth, Centaurs have a human upper half of torso and arms, and the lower body and legs of a horse. When Philyra saw Chiron, she was so shocked and disgusted that she turned herself into a tree. Chiron was abandoned: he was rejected by his mother and never knew his father.

Apollo, god of music, poetry and healing, became his foster father, and taught Chiron many skills. Under his tuition, Chiron became a wise man.

One evening, Chiron was attending a Centaurs' dinner, when Hercules paid a visit. A row erupted in the vast dining hall, and an enraged Hercules began to fight with the Centaurs. The Centaurs scattered in all directions, pursued by Hercules who fired his poisoned arrows at them. One of the arrows hit Chiron in the leg, and created a terrible wound which would never heal.

Chiron suffered from his injury for the rest of his life. His healing skills could not cure it. Because he was an immortal god, he could not die from the wound, and was destined to a life of eternal pain.

Chiron became a great healer nevertheless. One of his most celebrated patients was Telephus, who had been wounded by a spear that Chiron himself had made for his friend King Peleus. When Telephus consulted the oracle of Apollo, he was told that the wound could only be healed by its cause. Only Chiron – the cause of the wound – could cure him, and he did.

Although Chiron's own wound would not heal, he was given hope of relief. As punishment for bringing fire to humans, Prometheus had been bound to a rock by Zeus. Every day, a griffon swooped down to the rock and pecked at Prometheus' liver. Zeus decreed that Prometheus could only be released if an immortal agreed to take his place and give up his immortality.

Hercules, who had injured Chiron, pleaded Chiron's case to Zeus, who agreed to Hercules' request. Chiron took Prometheus' place on the rock, where he eventually died and was relieved of his suffering. Hercules shot the terrible Griffon through the head.

- The cycles in the plot create patterns of wholeness and completion. Hercules, like Chiron, becomes both wounder and healer.
- The characters remain consistent throughout the narrative: Hercules is a force of strength and aggression, which can be channelled for good or ill, and Chiron is a noble figure who rises above adversity to do good.
- The griffon, the spear and the wound are vivid symbols that resonate deep in the mind.

Choose books that relate closely to your moods, and stories that can transform the perspective you have on the world now, to one that will give you fresh opportunities and viewpoints. Here are some suggestions.

- *The Velveteen Rabbit* by Margery Williams – an enormously compassionate children's story.
- *The Count of Monte Cristo* by Alexandre Dumas – a grand story of revenge and redemption.
- *Cinderella* – perhaps the ultimate story of justice prevailing in the end.
- *A Scanner Darkly* by Philip K. Dick – the science fiction master is primarily concerned with human decency against a background of degradation and squalor.
- *The Cider House Rules* by John Irving – as with many of Irving's books, an awful situation is worked into something good.
- *Jonathan Livingston Seagull* by Richard Bach – an uplifting story created from deceptively simple symbols.
- *A Malgudi Omnibus* by R. K. Narayan – the fictional town of Malgudi illustrates real human feelings and values.

CASE STUDY

Laura is a single woman in her sixties, who suffered from severe bouts of depression. She was often irascible in the company of her friends, who at times described her as 'impossible'. When she began writing therapy, she was scornful and cynical. Writing her autobiography was a difficult process, as she discovered events in her childhood that she had suppressed, and which were very painful to voice. Gradually, she found she was able to

relate these childhood events to the way she behaved now towards other people. She gained understanding and insights that helped her to become more stable. In addition, she surprised herself and impressed her therapist with her writing ability.

THREE STORIES

Read through the three stories below and think about which one appeals to you most, and why.

1) A stonecutter wants to break apart a giant boulder. He takes a large hammer and smashes the boulder as hard as he can. The first time he hits it, he makes no impression: not even a scratch or a dent. He lifts up the hammer and hits it again. He makes no mark. He strikes it again and again and again – one hundred, two hundred times, without making a scratch – but the stonecutter persists. Passers-by laugh at him for because his actions seem to have no effect, but he carries on regardless.

   Suddenly, the boulder splits in half. Is it a single strike that breaks the stone? No. It is the constant and continual process applied to the challenge at hand.

   The application of discipline is the hammer that can break open any boulder that impedes your progress.

2) Thomas Edison tried thousands and thousands of times to perfect the filament for the light bulb. A reporter asked him how he could continue after so many failures. Edison replied: 'I never failed. On each occasion I discovered one more way not to invent the light bulb.'

3) Napoleon Hill in his classic motivational text *Think and Grow Rich* tells of the uncle of one R. U. Darby. One day this uncle set off to dig for gold. He staked his claim over an area of land and went to work with a pick and shovel.

After weeks of labour, he discovered a line of shining gold. Quickly, he covered up his mine, and rushed home to Williamsburg, Maryland, to tell his relatives and a few neighbours about his strike. They collected money for machinery to bring the gold to the surface. Then he returned with his nephew to work the mine.

The first car of ore was mined and shipped to a smelter. The smelted returns proved the uncle now owned one of the richest mines in Colorado. Only a few more cars of ore would clear his debts, then the big profits would roll in. The drills went down and his hopes went up.

Then the vein of gold disappeared. Though Darby and his uncle drilled further, they found no more gold.

So they quit. They sold the machinery to a junk merchant for a few hundred dollars and despondently took the train home.

The junk merchant called in an engineer to examine the mine and do some calculations. The engineer advised him that the project had failed because the owners were unfamiliar with fault lines. His calculations showed that the vein of gold was just one metre from where the nephew and uncle had stopped drilling.

That was exactly where the gold was found. The junk merchant took millions of dollars' worth of gold from the mine because he sought expert counsel.

Many years later, R. U. Darby used his experience as a lesson, and vowed that he would never stop because others say there is no point in going on. He recouped his loss many times over by selling more than a million dollars of life insurance annually.

These stories illustrate a common theme in different ways: that of persistence triumphing over adversity. They all give advice, and lock it into the emotions through vivid imagery. The pattern suggests that success is just around the corner.

Which symbols worked best for you? The image of the boulder smashing, Thomas Edison, or the lesson of the gold mine? Find what best connects the stories to your life, so you persist and triumph, despite obstacles.

EXERCISES

The following exercises explore narrative, action, characterization, surprise, and description.

- This visualization was used with a therapy group at Greenwich District Hospital. Try it, and see what images form in your mind.

You are going on an important journey. Before you start, you choose three tools to assist you when you encounter obstacles. Take what comes to you instinctively, no matter how silly or impractical it might seem. Visualize the three pieces of equipment clearly.

You begin your journey at the base of a tall mountain. It is spring and the air is clear and fresh. You start to walk up – the slope is gentle at this point. Is it covered in vegetation or barren? How do you see the mountain? Notice the rock the mountain is made of, and how high the mountain is. See the animals on the lower slopes. Feel the pleasant, calm, soothing air around you.

You continue to walk up the mountain. It becomes steeper, and demands more effort from you as you ascend. You encounter the first obstacle. Somehow, one of your tools will help you to overcome it. Delight in the feeling of success as you conquer the obstacle.

Continue to ascend the mountain. Focus on the goal, which is to reach the top, but be aware of the beauty of the natural landscape around you. The sun is shining and the air is warm.

You approach a second obstacle, and use a second tool to over-come it. Take as long as you need. When you have overcome the obstacle, focus on your feelings of success as you continue on your way up.

You climb further up the mountain. It is steep and rocky, but the exertion energizes you and makes you feel good. There are no animals up here. You can see the summit. You carry on climbing up. Just before the pinnacle, you encounter a third obstacle.

Using your third tool, you overcome this obstruction. Take as long as you need. When you have mastered it, feel once again all the sensations of success.

Continue your ascent to the summit. It is very high up, and quiet. Congratulate yourself on reaching this height. Enjoy all the feelings of success, mastery and power. Know that you can use these feelings whenever you need to surmount obstacles in any area of your life. Take the time to survey the panoramic view. Feel and enjoy the breeze. An unusual shrub grows on the summit, with brightly coloured flowers. They send out a delicious scent.

When you are ready, return at a leisurely pace down the moun-tain. Notice where you have been, and recall any feelings of apprehension you had, and how good it feels to have conquered them. You pass the third obstacle, and as you continue down the mountain, you notice more clearly the surrounding landscape and even other mountains stretching far into the distance. Now you pass what was once the second obstacle. Notice how much smaller it seems than before. Recall how it felt to face it, then how you overcame it. And now, on your journey down the mountain-side, you pass the first obstacle.

Take a moment to realize that you have completed your jour-ney up and down the mountain. In a sense, you are back where you began, but think of what you have gained: the knowledge that you can succeed and overcome all obstacles. You can make use of this understanding again and again.

PRINCIPLES OF ART THERAPIES

In the workshop, people had a massive assortment of images. Gladys, a widow, had the image of a mountain that she used to love climbing up with her husband. She carried the image in her mind after she left the group, and weeks later she described how the mountain had become a symbol that helped her get through the day. At times of stress or fear she focused on the image and gained strength.

- Make an amazing story out of something trivial that has happened to you or a friend during the last week. Write it down, then examine your narrative. What would enliven it and make it utterly compelling?

  Master of anecdotes and storytelling David Niven used to tell his stories over and over again, and it is said that every time he told a story, it improved.

- Choose five fundamental, defining events in your life. Consider what effects they have had on you, good and bad. Is there an underlying connection between the events? Can you find a thread to link them all up?

- You are on one island and your loved one is on another. The two islands are separated by a great choppy sea in which rages a storm. Look into the gale. How strong is it? How threatening?

  Build a bridge between the islands, or launch a boat to travel across. Describe the construction of the bridge, or the voyage in your boat. Try combining different modalities: remember, in the mind anything is possible. Really use your imagination. For example, how would you build such a bridge out of music?

- Design your perfect day. As in the movie *Groundhog Day*, you have the chance to devise exactly what you would do in your ideal world. Write out the agenda for the entire day

from the moment you wake up to when you fall asleep. Be
specific, and have fun – this is your best day!

This exercise can lead you to devise goals, set in motion means for achieving them, and initiate your actions towards these means. You are halfway there already!

- Write a short summary of a difficult situation in the past that you turned to your advantage. Now focus on a problem that you currently face. Write it down using not more than four lines, then write down the opportunities the problem presents. Describe ways in which it can lead you achieve greater success than you would have without it.

- Think about how you could turn the worst moment of your life into something good. Carl Jung developed the alchemy metaphor for turning dross into pure gold.

If you are feeling very unhappy, this exercise might seem impossible. Begin by telling a story about someone else, real or imaginary, and how they overcome their difficulty. Then apply it to yourself.

- Finish this story:

For a very long time, I have carried a great burden with me wherever I have gone. This heavy load has often tired me. Other people have never understood the weight I have had to carry. Now I am travelling to a place where I will finally be able to leave this burden. I am about to let go …

A woman crying in her suffering and unable to accept the death of her husband approached the Buddha. He directed her to boil a piece of arrowroot obtained from any family in which no man had ever died.

Deranged with grief, she rushed to the nearest town and knocked on door after door. She wandered from house to house until eventually, after talking to each house owner and listening to their sufferings, she realized that she was not alone in her grief. Her despair was universal and others had learned to live with it. She found herself able to bear her pain.

MULTIMEDIA
IN ART THERAPIES

Where the danger is, lies the saving power also.

HOLDERLIN, FROM 'THE RHINE'

Today, multimedia technology can be used to detect and assess your emotional state, and then help you to change it.

Dr Elizabeth Stroelbel is a psychologist at Ultramind. This company specializes in bio-medical interfaces. It has developed a game called 'Evolve', in which narrative, music and pictures respond to the user's physiology. The system has been successfully used with clients suffering from disorders ranging from headaches to irritable bowel syndrome. An animated fish swims to music through a colourful underwater landscape on the screen, while sensors detect your state of tension or relaxation. As you relax, the animation on screen responds: the music softens and the fish transforms into a mermaid, a powerful symbol which you can lock into your mind. Afterwards, when you are no longer using the hardware interface, you can visualize the mermaid in your imagination as a pathway back into the relaxed state. Dr Stroelbel is currently working on extending the application of these real-time processing and feedback techniques.

Multimedia also offers new possibilities for storytelling and drama: with interactive CD-ROMs, you can determine how characters respond in certain situations, and so how a story unfolds. If you are aware that the way you respond affects the drama, you will notice your reactions.

Imagine a viewing of your favourite film in which the audience controls the outcome. The possibilities are interesting: if the audience becomes extremely sad, the computer can script a happier ending.

Computers offer opportunities to experiment with and develop creative work in new ways. Scanners, graphics tablets (programs which allow you to draw with your computer using a pen instead of a mouse), and CD-ROMs enable you to create, manipulate and organize images, in colour, black and white, in two or three dimensions.

CASE STUDIES

Kaleidoscope is an organization working with people in mental distress to produce computer-generated art. One man in his fifties was very cut off from his feelings. Using a computer graphics system he began painting trees and scenes from his childhood, and began to access his emotions. Similarly, another client, Mary, used computers to integrate text and images to express how she was feeling after a breakdown. She now feels much more confident, and has benefited from organizing and expressing her feelings through multimedia using music, speech and graphics. She intends to continue developing her art using multimedia, and helps others to gain similar benefits.

The Internet offers new scope for communicating images, words and sounds with people across the world. In the space of only a few years, electronic communication has become commonplace, even for 'technophobes'. I believe that the possibilities for art therapies are only just beginning. If you have e-mail, you can already share sounds and images. A variety of user groups that are updated daily can be found with a simple search on Worldwide Web. This means that someone in America can share a soundfile of a poem with a person in Japan.

In the future, computers will assist in designing therapeutic artworks. They will not merely assist in techniques of expression (e.g. refining a colour palette, or making musical notation easier to understand). Computers will be able to pick up emotional patterns of the user and coordinate relevant enhanced therapeutic symbols that the user had not thought of. It is early days, but there is enormous potential to develop interactive art therapies using words, images and musical sounds.

THE ART OF
SUCCESSFUL LIVING

The book should be a ball of light in one's hand.

EZRA POUND

Arts can help you to feel better about yourself and generate changes in your life. Painting, music, drama, stories and poetry can be applied to a variety of life situations.

Art forms mediate between the world of your dreams and the outside world. They enable you to make sense of the inner world, and give you a symbolic language with which to access your depths, release energy, and provide new ways of looking at the world and facing your emotions.

Yet if the arts have the power to heal, they also have the power to harm. It is therefore important to consider carefully the effects of the arts in our culture. In many homes a television blasts out an unchecked stream of sounds, images and stories. Soap operas, comedies, documentaries, horror movies, thrillers, news programmes, games shows, sports and commercials pour a bewildering amount of information into our brains. Most of us are not taught how to process this mass of information, and we can become confused.

We do not have a coherent concept of what it does to us. We must think about the effect of a harrowing documentary on a

child; of violent and horror films on a psychotically disturbed person; and of a daily intake of mostly downbeat news stories on the world.

Freedom of expression is profoundly important, but it is worrying that disturbing sounds, images and films are everywhere, while the means to cope with them are not. True: a film devoted to the theme of hatred can be therapeutic – when distressing emotions are contained in a work, the audience knows they are not alone in pain and suffering – but it needs to be safely contained. If it is not, it can leave people disturbed, vulnerable and even dangerous.

It does not suffice to dismiss art forms as reflections of society. Oscar Wilde famously said in a phrase with more depth than repartee, that: 'Life imitates art far more than art imitates life.'

We should educate ourselves by opening up a dialogue with our friends and families after watching something that may have been disturbing. And I believe that we should be taught more formally about how our emotions work. This would provide a framework for processing our feelings.

The healing process gives your life form and harmony, allowing dissonant elements – anger and love, sadness and joy, togetherness and solitude, acceptance and rejection, self and other – to come together in a balanced whole.

Take the opportunity to use the arts to shape your life in the way that you desire, and fill your life with energy, passion, creativity and fun. You are what you are, yet you can be what you want to be. You cannot take away what has happened to you, but by looking at your past through a world of symbols, you can redesign the significance of events, and give them a context that makes sense. Finding order in things, beyond the surface pain, taking the worst events of your life and shaping them into something good: that, I believe, is making your life into a work of art.

PRINCIPLES OF ART THERAPIES

RESOURCES

GENERAL

BOOKS AND JOURNALS

Cameron, Julia. *The Artist's Way: Spiritual Path to Higher Creativity*, Souvenir Press, 1994

Dr Delaney, Gayle. *Sexual Dreams: Why We Have Them and What They Mean*, Piatkus Books, 1994

Gawain, Shakti. *Creative Visualization: Use the Power of Your Imagination to Create*, Bantam Boooks, 1987

Henri, Robert. *The Art Spirit*, Harper & Row, 1984

Linn, Denise. *Pocketful of Dreams*, Piatkus Books, 1997

O'Connor, Joseph and McDermott, Ian. *Principles of NLP*, Thorsons, 1996

Reid, Lori. *The Dream Catcher: Unravel the Mysteries of Your Sleeping Mind*, Element Books, 1997

Jessica Kingsley Publishers offer a wide choice of books on art therapies:
118 Pentonville Road
London N1 9JN

Artery: Journal of Arts for Health
Manchester Metropolitan University
All Saints
Oxford Road
Manchester M15 6BH
Tel: 0161 236 8916

Hospice Arts Journal
c/o Forbes House
9 Artillery Lane
London E1 7LP
Tel: 01245 358130

USEFUL ADDRESSES

Contact the organizations below for information about workshops and courses in your area.

Arts Council of Great Britain
14 Great Peter Street
London SW1P 3NQ
Tel: 0171 333 0100
Fax: 0171 973 6590

Artlink: Arts for people with disabilities
The Guildhall Centre
St Peters Hill
Grantham
Lincolnshire
Tel: 01476 592284

PAINTING

BOOKS

Edwards, Betty. *Drawing on the Right Side of the Brain*, HarperCollins, 1993

Dalley, Tessa. *Art as Therapy: An Introduction to the Use of Art as a Therapeutic Technique*, Routledge, 1990

USEFUL ADDRESSES

British Association of Art Therapists
13C Northwood Road
London N6

Conquest (Society for Art for Physically Handicapped People)
3 Beverley Close
East Ewell
Epsom
Surrey KT17 3HB
Tel: 0181 393 6102

MUSIC

BOOKS

Dewhurst-Maddox, Olivea. *Healing with Sound: Self-help Techniques Using Music and Your Voice*, Gaia Books, 1997

Ansdell, Gary. *Music for Life: Aspects of Creative Music Therapy with Adult Clients*, Jessica Kingsley Publishers, 1995

Community Music
Interchange Studios
Dalby Streeet
London NW5 3NQ

British Society for Music Therapy
69 Avondale Avenue
East Barnet
Hertfordshire EN4 8NB

National Music and Disability Information Service
Riverside House
Rattlesden
Bury St Edmunds
IP30 0SF
Tel: 01449 736287

DRAMA

BOOKS

Grainger, Roger. *Drama and Healing: The Roots of Drama Therapy*, Jessica Kingsley Publishers, 1990
Jennings, Sue. *Dramatherapy: Theory and Practice for Teachers and Clinicians*, Routledge, 1988

Age Exchange Theatre Trust
The Reminiscence Centre
11 Blackheath Village
London SE3 9LA
Tel: 0181 318 9105

National Association of Dramatherapy (USA)
19 Edwards Street
New Haven
Connecticutt 06511

British Association for Dramatherapists
P.O. Box 98
Kirbymoorside
Yorks YO6 6EX

POETRY

BOOKS

Duffy, Carol Ann, ed. *Stopping for Death: Poems of Death and Loss*, Viking Children's Books, 1996
Quiller-Couch, Arthur, ed. *The Oxford Book of English Verse*, Oxford University Press, 1990

USEFUL ADDRESSES

Contact the organizations below for information about workshops and courses in your area.
Survivors Poetry
34 Osnaburgh Streeet
London NW1 3ND
Tel: 0171 916 5317

Poetry Society of America
15 Granmercy Park
New York
NY 10003
Tel: 212 254 9628

Academy of American Poets
584 Broadway
Suite 1208
New York
NY 10012–3250
Tel: 212 274 0343

STORIES

BOOKS

Jackowska, Nicki. *Write for Life*, Element Books, 1997
Rowshan, Arthur. *Telling Tales: How to Use Stories to Help Children Overcome Their Problems*, Element, 1997

USEFUL ADDRESSES

REACH (National Library for Handicapped Children)
Sistine Manor
Stoke Green
Stoke Poges
Bucks SL2 4HT
Tel: 01753 578018

c/o Poetry Society
22 Betterton Street
London WC2H 9BU
Tel: 0171 240 4910

MULTIMEDIA

USEFUL ADDRESSES

Ultramind UK
2 Lindsey Street
London EC1A 9HP
Tel 0171 677 7000
E-mail: london@ultramind.co.uk

Channel Cyberia
http://channel.cyberiacafe.net

National Council for Education Technology
Milburn Hill Road
Science Park
Coventry CV4 7JJ
Tel: 01203 416994

Inclusive Technology
Tel: 0161 835 3677
http://www.inclusive.co.uk

PRINCIPLES OF ART THERAPIES